D0886833

Nelson and Sea Power

NELSON and Sea Power

Christopher Lloyd

The English Universities Press Ltd

ISBN 0 340 12413 X

First published 1973

The English Universities Press Ltd
St Paul's House, Warwick Lane, London EC4P 4AH
Battle plans drawn by Crispin Fisher
Printed in Great Britain by Hazell Watson & Viney Ltd
Aylesbury, Bucks

Introduction to the Series

This series has been undertaken in the conviction that no sub-ject is more important than history. For though the conquests of natural science (nuclear fission, the exploration of space, genetic advance, bacteriology, etc.) have given their character to the age, it is actually a greater need to gain control of the forces of nature loosed upon us. The prime urgency, the deepest neces-sity is in the human field: to understand the nature and condi-tion of man as a pre-condition of better controls, and fewer disasters, in the world of politics and society.

There is no better introduction to this sphere, and the un-derstanding of its problems, than history. *Some* knowledge of history, we feel, ought to prevent some mistakes: at every point we can learn vicariously from the experience of others before us.

To take one point only – the understanding of politics: how can we understand the world of affairs around us, if we do not know how it came to be what it is? How to interpret the United States, or Soviet Russia, France, Germany or Britain without some knowledge of their history?

Some evidence of the growing awareness of this may be seen in the great increase of interest in history among the general public, and in the much larger place the subject has come to take in education.

The most congenial, as well as the most concrete and prac-tical, approach to history is the biographical: through the lives of great men whose careers have been significant in history. Fashions in historical writing have their ups and downs; men's and women's lives have their perennial interest – though in this series we are chiefly concerned to show their historical significance, the contribution they made to their age: *Men and their Times*.

A generation ago historical biographies were rather un-fashionable with analytical historians and technicians, like Namier: he ended by writing scores of miniature biographies of M.P.s. The detailed analysis of Civil War and Commonwealth has ended by showing that there were almost as many party-divisions as there were individuals. We are back in the realm of biography and the biographical approach to history, since there is no greater diversity, variety and subtlety than in the lives of individual men and women, particularly those who left a mark on their time.

A. L. ROWSE
All Souls College, Oxford

Contents

Battle Plans

Plates

Acknowledgments

The author and publisher wish to thank the following for permission to reproduce the illustrations in this book: the National Maritime Museum, Greenwich, plates I, II, III, IV, VI, VII, VIII, IX; the National Portrait Gallery, plate V (on loan from the Leggatt Tustees).

1   Apprenticeship

In the summer of the year 1776 Midshipman Horatio Nelson, aged eighteen, lay shivering in his hammock on board the *Seahorse* frigate in the Hoogli river below Calcutta. He was suffering from what was generally called fever, probably malaria, and because the ship was so small no Peruvian bark was carried on board to cure it. His frame was reduced to a skeleton, his brown hair turning grey and his spirits so depressed that even he was convinced that he would never rise in his profession. 'After a long and gloomy reverie in which I almost wished myself overboard, a sudden glow of patriotism was kindled within me. "Well then," I exclaimed, "I will be a hero and, confiding in Providence, I will brave every danger!" '

Two years previously he had nearly lost his life in the Arctic, where his captain had seen the boy beating a polar bear about the head with his musket on an ice flow. A few years later he was invalided home from the West Indies (as he had been from India) on the point of death after an attack of yellow fever. He was lucky to reach the age of manhood without losing his life from some fatal disease attendant on the exigencies of the service in every type of climate. And, when war began, he was to prove himself accident-prone, an unfortunate failing in a fighting man. In nearly every action he was seriously wounded, until he was finally killed in battle. Even when he suffered his first wound in Corsica he could say, 'I have all the diseases that are, but there is not enough in my frame for them to fasten on'. No wonder it was he who said that 'the great thing in all military service is health'. If ever a man proved an example of the triumph of mind over matter, of ardent ambition over every physical disability, it was Nelson.

'What has poor Horatio done, who is so weak, that above all the rest he should be sent to rough it at sea?' asked his uncle when he agreed to take him on board his ship at the age of twelve. 'But let him come; and the first time we go into action a cannon ball may knock off his head and so provide for him.'

It was family necessity that made his father send the delicately built boy to sea. The Rev. Edmund Nelson, rector of Burnham Thorpe in Norfolk for forty-six years, had been left to care for eight children on the death of his wife nine years after Horatio, her sixth child out of a family of eleven, was born on 29 September 1758. Apart from his father, both Nelson's grandfathers and two of his brothers were clergymen. They were a dim, respectable, middle-class East Anglian family, without any important relations apart from a distant connection with the Walpole family, so that it was from the second Lord Walpole that Horatio took his name, not from the better known Horace Walpole of Strawberry Hill.

His only recollection of his mother was that she 'hated the French'. Her son inherited the prejudice. When staying in France to learn the language (which he never succeeded in doing), long before the Revolutionary wars began, he confessed that, 'I hate this country and their manners'. With his highly emotional temperament, it was a feeling which animated all his dealings with them. Xenophobia was a marked characteristic with him: he despised the Spaniards and the Portuguese, but he hated the French. Since he spent the greater part of his life fighting them, perhaps it was as well that he did so.

The early death of his mother may have affected him in other ways. There is a strong feminine streak in his character, an emotional need for affection and tenderness, which the brutal life on board ship could never satisfy. It explains the depth of his friendship with more self-sufficient men like Collingwood and Troubridge, who loved him personally even more than they respected his abilities. It helps to account for the failure of his marriage to a cold woman, who lavished her affections on her son rather than on her husband. The secret of Emma Hamilton's hold over him was that she not only loved but nursed and flattered him.

His father delighted to bask in the glory of the genius which so surprisingly developed in his son. The relations between the two were conventional. The son wrote dutiful letters to his father, the father passed on the news to the rest of the family, for whom Nelson had no particular regard. The father, in his old age, was the only man who was accepted both by Nelson's wife and by his mistress, yet when he died in 1802 Nelson did not attend his funeral, though he paid for it. As he wrote to his elder brother, 'My state of health and what my feelings would naturally be, might be of serious consequence to myself'. One gets the impression that Emma might have dictated that letter.

The most important assets for advancement in eighteenth-century life were wealth and 'interest'. The only useful connection which the family possessed was Mrs Nelson's brother, Maurice Suckling, a captain in the Navy who rose to the influential position of Comptroller on the Navy Board. It was therefore Captain Suckling who placed the eldest Nelson boy in the Navy Office as a clerk, and who agreed to take the third surviving son, Horatio, on board his line-of-battle ship *Raisonable* in 1770, where he was rated a midshipman at the age of twelve years and three months.

The age of entry had been fixed at thirteen by the regulations of 1731, but eighteenth-century regulations were made to be broken. As we shall see, Nelson broke all of them – administrative, tactical and social. Normally, a boy entered the service as a 'captain's servant', a relic of the old apprenticeship system which permitted the captain of a ship to take on board a certain number of followers. He should not have been rated a midshipman until he had served four years at sea. Only a handful of officers joined as such direct from the Naval Academy at Portsmouth, the vast majority being protégés of captains and variously rated as captain's servant, midshipman or able seaman, as was Nelson; in 1794 the first of these titles was changed to that of Volunteer, First Class, the second class volunteers becoming genuine seamen when they grew up. There was a widespread practice among potential officers of making false musters, in order to gain the nominal six years' service before taking the Lieutenant's examination at the minimum age of twenty. Collingwood's first lieutenant at Trafalgar had been entered on the ship's books at the age of one. At seventeen Cochrane, later Earl of Dundonald, was a midshipman on no less than three ships as well as holding a commission in the Guards.

There was one thing to be said for recruiting naval officers in this way : they learned their responsibilities young, and they could not buy their commissions. There was no 'purchase' system in the Navy such as that which prevailed in the Army, largely because the king's ships were far too valuable to be left to the care of amateurs. Whereas a lieutenant-colonel paid £6,700 for a commission in the Guards without any previous experience, a Post-Captain of a line-of-battle ship had come up the hard way, even though his examination to 'pass for lieutenant' was a formality. There were, indeed, midshipmen who could not pass even this simple test in navigation and therefore spent the rest of their lives as 'oldsters' compared with the genuine midshipmen known as 'youngsters' or 'young gentlemen'. Such pathetic, grey haired midshipmen certainly knew their seamanship, even though they were hardly literate.

Because he left school at the age of twelve, it is hardly surprising that Nelson had few interests apart from the sea. He was not well read, he took little interest in politics and none in the arts. In spite of being intensely ambitious, he was not interested in money, beyond demanding (sometimes at law) what he regarded as his just share of prize money, and even that because advancement in his profession was ever uppermost in his mind. At Norwich Grammar School he received the usual rudiments of a classical education at the hands of Classic Jones, described by a schoolfellow as 'as keen a flogger as the merciless Busby, of birch-loving memory'. Yet no man has ever written better letters. From his vast correspondence, so piously collected in seven volumes by Sir Harris Nicolas and by later editors, we know him better than any other historical personage because he wrote so spontaneously. Official letters were of course written to a formula, as they still are, but in Nelson's personal letters he wears his heart upon his sleeve. Never was a man so open on paper, and never were so many letters written in so natural a style or so free from snide comments, for he was a generous-hearted man.

Men grew up quickly in the school of life in those days. Wellington, who entered the Army at seventeen, was a Lieutenant-Colonel at twenty-four. Pitt was Prime Minister at twenty-four. Nelson passed his Lieutenant's examination at eighteen (though he should have been twenty). He was a Captain at twenty, and when a government official at Jamaica told him 'that old Generals were not in the habit of taking advice from young gentlemen', he replied: 'I have the honour, Sir, of being as old as the Prime Minister of England, and think myself as capable of commanding one of his Majesty's ships as that Minister is of governing the State'.

Promotion as far as Captain was largely a matter of interest. Thereafter, though influence continued to count, opportunity, zeal and ability counted for more. As there were no arrangements for retirement, an officer went on half-pay when he was not employed at sea and could always be called upon to serve again until he finally retired underground. Promotion was strictly governed by seniority, hence the avid reading of Navy Lists and the wardroom toast of 'A bloody war or a sickly season'. To know who had died was a matter of prime professional interest. Nelson was lucky enough to live at a time when opportunity beckoned and when many an officer died young. Even so, he did not become a Rear-Admiral until he was thirty-eight. He died at forty-seven as a Vice-Admiral. To have become a full Admiral, or Admiral of the Red, he would have had to have lived until he was eighty-six, such was the survival rate of his seniors on the List of Sea Officers.

In any ship's company the executive officers were composed of 'officers and gentlemen': even George Washington was of the opinion that only a gentleman could command. The civilian officers – chaplains, surgeons, pursers – were not gentlemen, nor were they commissioned by their Lordships of the Admiralty in the same way. Between them and the warrant officers (masters, boatswains, gunners, masters-at-arms, etc.) an even greater social gulf was fixed. Very few like Captain Cook were promoted from being Master, i.e. navigating officer, on the Lower Deck to being an executive officer on the Quarter Deck, such was the professional and social gap between the two.

To become a warrant officer was thus the peak of promotion to which a member of 'the People' could aspire. Over half the seamen in any ship never wanted to be at sea at all: they were pressed men, though they lived the same kind of life as the volunteer seamen. Most of the latter had entered the service as boys and were able, as compared with ordinary, seamen. After the passing of the Quota Acts in 1794 on account of difficulties in manning the Navy to fight the long war with France, a large proportion of the crew were either foreigners or unskilled landmen (later called 'landsmen'), forming an element in the ship's company which was as much despised on account of its lack of seamanlike qualities as were 'the people' in general by the officers of a superior social class.

After he had been a few months on board the *Raisonable*, Captain Suckling sent the young Horatio on a voyage to the West Indies in a merchant ship, while quite illegally retaining his name on the books of a warship in order to draw his pay. 'I returned,' says Nelson in an autobiographical sketch, 'a practical seaman, with a horror of the Royal Navy, and with a saying then constant with seamen, "Aft the most honour, forward the better man".'

There was no love lost between merchant seamen and the Navy. Owners disliked sailing in convoy as much as naval officers did, and as for the men, impressment had been the accepted method of manning the fleet for centuries. There was a hard core of volunteers and prime seamen, but the majority had been pressed into the service because they 'used the sea' as a profession. Men of such a way of life could be legally conscripted, except when they were apprentices, householders or fishermen, who carried a passport of exemption known as a 'protection'. Only when one considers the size of the Navy in Nelson's day can one appreciate the desperate efforts of the press gangs and the Impress Service to round up able-bodied men, often petty criminals, to solve the problem of manning the fleet. Five years after Nelson had won the war at sea, when Wellington was leading the Peninsular Army in Spain, there were 142,098 men in sea pay, 23,455 Sea Fencibles (a type of naval militia), 20,000 privateersmen exempt from naval service, together with an Army of over 200,000, out of a total population of England and Wales of only 8 million. The fact that Jane Austen hardly mentions the Napoleonic wars in her novels should not obscure the strain on the nation's manpower which twenty years of war involved.

It was not lack of patriotism, nor even the strict discipline necessary to control such heterogeneous crews which kept men from joining the Navy, or, what was worse, deserting it at the first opportunity. Life was hard enough on shore, and punishments for breaking the criminal code just as brutal. It was the lack of liberty, the denial of shore leave which was essential to prevent desertion, and the low pay, which gave the Navy such a bad name. Any man could earn twice as much on board the smallest merchant ship in wartime as the 24/- a month offered to able seamen by the Navy. The rate of pay had remained unchanged since the days of Cromwell, and the pittance was not paid until a ship was paid off, sometimes years after a man had joined her. Even then payment was often made by wage tickets which had to be cashed at a discount. Nor was the statutory amount actually paid in full: there were deductions of sixpence a month for the maintenance of Greenwich Hospital (though a man was lucky if he ever reached it), fourpence to supplement the pay of the chaplain, and twopence for the surgeon.

It is typical of Nelson that after his first ship was paid off he took the trouble to go to London to collect the pay due to his men. Like other captains, he regularly employed gangs to fill the complement of his ships, but unlike the more tyrannical type of commander he could always rely on a substantial number of men following him from ship to ship if they were given the opportunity. According to him, 'disgust of the seamen to the navy is all owing to the infernal plan of turning them over from ship to ship, so that men cannot be attached to their officers, or the officers care twopence about them'. He is alluding to the wartime practice, by which men were not allowed on shore at a home port in case they deserted.

An equally iniquitous practice was to press men in the Downs out of merchant ships returning from a long voyage, the crews of outward bound vessels being usually exempt because of the uproar made in Parliament by those representing the powerful East or West Indian interests. Until the middle of the nineteenth century, Britain never had a standing Navy any more than she had a standing Army. It is true that the Navy was more favoured because it was less of a political hazard, and that ships and officers were retained, but as soon as a ship was paid off, or as soon as hostilities ended, official responsibility for the men ceased – until they had to be pressed again. Such was the hire-and-discharge system which prevented the growth of a regular naval service.

Naval officers disliked this haphazard method of manning, not only because it was inefficient, but because it was manifestly unjust and gave the service a bad name. The legend of the jolly tar standing as a bulwark to British liberty is largely a post-Nelsonian attitude, and the sincerest tribute which the men paid him as an officer was the number of occasions on which they petitioned to serve under him in a new ship. But this could never solve the problem on a national scale, and when a long war necessitated the forcible impressment of tens of thousands of men the problem of leadership became acute. A heterogeneous crew could be flogged into shape in a few months, but the men deserted at the first opportunity. Until a satisfactory officer–man relationship was evolved, the problem remained insoluble. Until then, most captains ruled by fear of the lash and only those like Nelson could inspire men to follow them with something like love.

The first steps to improve this state of affairs were taken when Nelson was a young man with the introduction of the divisional system, by which crews were divided up into groups under the supervision of a lieutenant. Some personal relationship and responsibility was then established, instead of ruling a mob by the continual exercise of the cat-o'-nine-tails, or the rattan for an unofficial 'starting'. A few improvements in pay and victualling were made after the fleet mutinies in 1797, which were strikes against the intolerable conditions prevailing at sea; but it was not until after the long wars were over and the fleet was reduced to a manageable size that radical reforms were possible and the end of impressment was in sight.

The seamen of Nelson's day may have been badly paid, badly fed, badly housed and badly treated, but they fought magnificently. The reason was good leadership in the widest sense of the word. By the example of his victories seamen felt, for the first time in history, that they mattered to the nation, and the nation (though it did little to improve their lot) honoured them for what they did. It was Nelson's best service to his profession that he made the men in it greater than they were.

2 The Young Captain

Nelson passed his Lieutenant's examination in 1777. His uncle was on the board but tactfully refrained from mentioning his relationship to the candidate until all was over. The certificate, dated 9 April, states that he 'appears to be more than 20 years of age ... and can splice, knot, reef a sail, etc., and is qualified to do the duty of an Able Seaman or a Midshipman'. In point of fact he was hardly nineteen, looked like a boy, and for years past had performed such duties to everyone's satisfaction. But 'passing for lieutenant' meant that his apprenticeship was over and that, as he told his brother, 'I am now left in the world to shift for myself'.

The next day he was appointed to the *Lowestoffe*, a 32-gun frigate whose captain, William Locker, became a friend for life.* Nelson's first necessary but unpleasant duty was to press men for the frigate and to open a rendezvous near the Tower of London where men could volunteer and where those pressed could be locked up until the ship sailed.

The War of American Independence was now no longer confined to America, though it did not become a world war until the entry of France and Spain in 1778. Nelson saw little actual

---

*Locker later became Governor of Greenwich Hospital and it was from his family that John Charnock obtained materials for the earliest biography of Nelson, published in 1806. The author happens to possess the family copy of this work and in a pencilled note Locker's son states: 'This is not true. Charnock stole the volume of letters while in possession of W. Lodge, his request to publish them having already been refused by my Sister.' An interesting link with Lord Fisher, a Nelson idolator and the creator of the Edwardian navy, is that the Locker family crest on the binding carries the motto 'Fear God and Fear Nought'.

fighting at sea, and had no opportunity of studying fleet tactics in action until some time later. The ships he served in were all brigs or frigates, the type of ship engaged on convoy duties, not fleet actions. The outline of the war does not, therefore, concern us here: suffice it to say that it was fought with a disastrous disregard for the strategic principles which had proved so successful in the previous war. The hinge on which British naval strategy turned was the blockade of enemy fleets in European ports. When this was broken, French fleets annually descended on the West Indies and the American seaboard, where they assisted the rebels to final victory. Thus we find Nelson zealously manning the batteries for the defence of Jamaica when it was feared that D'Estaing's fleet might appear out to sea, or defending his convoys against privateers, the eighteenth-century equivalent of submarines as commerce raiders.

After a short while in the *Lowestoffe* he was transferred to the command of a smaller frigate, the *Hinchingbroke*, of 28 guns,* on the sudden death of her captain. This made him a Post-Captain, a lucky advancement at such an early age: 'I got my rank by a shot killing a Post-Captain, and I most sincerely hope I shall, when I go, go out of the World in the same way'.

To get one's first command at the age of twenty was a thrilling experience, even though there was little chance of fighting the French in the West Indies now that the war was coming to an end. It was there that he met his closest friend, Cuthbert Collingwood, ten years older than himself but, because he lacked influence, still only the captain of a smaller ship. It was the same throughout his life: Collingwood never had Nelson's luck, or his flair. He was always, as at Trafalgar, second in command. He showed an even stronger devotion to duty than his friend, never better displayed than during the dull years after Nelson's death when he succeeded him as commander-in-chief in the Mediterranean. In nearly every respect he was a complementary character, in build, temperament and appearance. He was a sturdy Northumbrian type, devoted to his family but

* A table of the rating and armament of warships will be found in the Appendix.

never a popular figure because he lacked Nelson's glamour as a leader of men, less brilliant or volatile, more of an introvert, and without the personal charm which did so much to forward Nelson's career.

For want of anything better to do, the two captains were told to take their little ships to accompany an absurd amphibious expedition sent to capture a Spanish fort at San Juan, a hundred miles up a river in Nicaragua, which no Englishman had penetrated since the days of the buccaneers. It was a pointless and disastrous exploit. Typical of the planning in that war, the tiny force descended on Central America just when the rains broke. The Mosquito Coast was a notorious hotbed of yellow fever. In one night 87 of Nelson's men succumbed and Collingwood says that he buried 180 out of 200 men in his own ship. Nelson, of course, was an early victim, so that he was invalided home on the point of death for the second time in his career.

Convalescence followed at Bath, as was often to be the case in the future. A pleasant story is told of the doctor who attended him. When he sent in his bill it was so remarkably small that Nelson protested. 'Pray, Captain Nelson, allow me to follow what I consider to be my professional duty', was the reply. 'Your illness, sir, has been brought on by serving your King and Country, and believe me, I love both too well to be able to receive any more'. *O si sic omnes.*

As soon as he recovered he was appointed to another 28-gun frigate, the *Albemarle*. As before, he was employed on convoy duty, this time to Quebec; and, as before, he fell ill, this time with scurvy. This disease, due to a vitamin deficiency from living off salt beef without vegetables, was the notorious curse of the sea and at no time were casualties higher than during this war. This was all the more shocking because forty years previously Dr James Lind of Haslar Hospital had proved by the first controlled dietetic experiment in history that oranges and lemons were a true specific. The Admiralty paid no attention to his advice, and even Captain Cook, who kept his men healthy by other means, advised against the supply of lemon juice on the grounds of expense. Consequently men suffered in tens of thousands during the American war. Nelson reporting to Locker on the outbreak in the *Albemarle* says that he and his officers had been living on salt beef for eight weeks (the disease usually declares itself in six), while the ship's company had not had a fresh meal for seven months. Had not Sir Gilbert Blane, a disciple of Lind, been able as a Commissioner for Sick and Wounded to persuade the Admiralty in 1795 to supply lemon juice after six weeks at sea on salt provisions, the whole strategy of close blockade would have been out of the question. As a result of Blane's action, scurvy was almost a forgotten disease in the fleets which Nelson commanded.

If a sufferer from scurvy is not too far gone with the disease he recovers remarkably quickly on a diet of fresh vegetables. Nelson was soon on his feet again and felt sufficiently well to fall in love with 'an amiable American' loyalist. Unfortunately, she was only sixteen years old, so that it was left to a new friend named Alexander Davison to save the young man from making a fool of himself. Davison was a well-to-do shipowner who later became Nelson's financial agent and confidant in London.

More influential friends were made when the ship reached New York. A fish-faced midshipman, to whom undue deference seemed to be paid (he happened to be Prince William Henry, later William IV) noticed a strange figure coming over the side of Lord Hood's flagship:

He appeared to be the merest boy of a Captain I ever beheld: and his dress was worthy of attention. He had on a full-laced uniform: his lank unpowdered hair was tied in a stiff Hessian tail, of an extraordinary length; the old-fashioned flaps of his waistcoat added to the general quaintness of his figure, and produced an appearance which particularly attracted my notice; for I had never seen anything like it before, nor could I imagine who he was, nor what he came about. My doubts, however, were removed when Lord Hood introduced me to him. There was something irresistibly pleasing in his address and conversation; and an enthusiasm, when speaking on professional subjects, which showed he was no common being.

Samuel, Lord Hood, made a deep impression on Nelson, who regarded him as the best officer in the navy. Yet it had recently been Hood and Graves between them who virtually lost America by the mess they made of their tactics at the battle of the Chesapeake, called by the Americans the battle of the Capes. Their failure to take advantage of a propitious situation to destroy the French fleet led to the surrender of the army under Cornwallis at Yorktown in October 1781, a disaster which really marks the end of the war in America. Out of this failure, and after the striking victory of Rodney and Hood over De Grasse at the battle of the Saints, when the enemy line was broken for the first time in a hundred years, a tactical revolution developed of which Nelson was the heir. He must be seen as the inheritor of a new style of fighting which was to break the paralysis from which set battles at sea suffered throughout the wars of the eighteenth century The tactical innovations which are the glory of his victories owe much to the example set by men like Hood and Howe whom he met at this time.

Hood graciously permitted the *Albemarle* to accompany his fleet back to the West Indies, but Nelson's ship was too small to take part in a fleet action. He was, however, put in command of a detachment of small ships to oust the French from an unimportant islet called Turks Island in the Bahamas. This expedition, for which he seems to have been personally responsible, was like its predecessor at San Juan one of the few failures of his career. It was, according to a critical lieutenant who took part in it, 'a ridiculous expedition, undertaken by a young man merely from the hope of seeing his name in the papers'. In any event, the war was nearly over. England had lost America, though Rodney's victory helped to save the rest of the British empire overseas. It was time to go home, where the *Albemarle* paid off in the summer of 1783.

After a brief interval during which he visited France in order to learn the language, Nelson was lucky enough to get another ship, the *Boreas* (28 guns). At the end of a war the Navy was always drastically reduced, the authorities bearing no responsibility for the ten of thousands of men suddenly loosed on the labour market. Thus between 1783 and 1784 the number in pay dropped from 107,446 to 39,268 because of the number of ships laid up 'in ordinary'.

Nelson's destination was the Leeward Islands, to which he was carrying the wife of the commander-in-chief, together with a bevy of midshipmen anxious to earn some sea time. He never cared for Admiral Sir Richard Hughes or his lady – 'I do not like him, he bows and scrapes too much for me; his wife has an eternal clack' – nor did he find in him the support which a senior officer should give to his subordinates when they carry out unpopular duties.

This was to enforce the Navigation Acts by apprehending American interlopers, a coastguard job which Nelson keenly disliked though he attacked it with his customary zeal, particularly after the sense of humiliation which he, like the rest of his countrymen, suffered after the late war. The Navigation Acts passed to protect British shipping and trade clearly laid down that 'all admirals and commanders of King's ships are authorized to make seizure of ships offending therein' by unlicensed trade with British colonies. The natural pattern of trade between the American continent and the Sugar Islands had led to a flourishing commerce between the two, which was resented even when the American colonists were British subjects. Now that they were foreigners, they had no right to continue this trade. Merchants and shipowners, of course, wished to continue as before, the Customs officers turning a blind eye, as did the Governors of the islands and the station Admiral. But Nelson and Collingwood (who also happened to be out there at this time) were determined to enforce the law as it stood.

As seizure followed seizure, tension mounted. Suits were filed against this naval busybody. He was confined to his ship for weeks on end to avoid arrest. He could not get the lawyers to give a clear ruling on the issue. He appealed for support to his admiral, only to receive a dusty answer. He wrote repeatedly to the Secretary of the Admiralty explaining what he was doing, but received no reply. As he said at great length with conscious rectitude, he considered he was doing his duty and also keeping at bay the infiltration of American influence which, in the event of another war with the French, placed the security of the islands in jeopardy. Echoing the sentiments of Lord Rodney during the last war, he wrote

The residents of these islands are American by connexion and by interest, and are inimical to Great Britain. They are as great rebels as ever were in America, had they the power to show it. . . . Whilst I have the honour to command an English man-of-war, I never shall allow myself to be subservient to the will of any Governor, nor co-operate with him in doing illegal acts.

All this was worrying enough to make him dislike the whole area. The headquarters of the Leeward Islands station was English Harbour at Antigua (recently restored to its eighteenth-century state for the benefit of American tourists). Nelson regarded it as 'an infernal hole'. Barbados in the Windward Islands was worse – 'Barbarous Island', he addressed his letters. 'Never, never, do I believe shall I get away from this destestable spot. Had I not seized any Americans, I should now have been with you; but I should have neglected my duty.'

The letter was addressed to Fanny Nisbet, the widow of a judge and now the housekeeper of the richest merchant in the island of Nevis. Nelson imagined that she was five years younger than he was. Actually she was a few months older, both of them being twenty-seven.

She had a son named Josiah aged five. Her figure was elegant, her complexion fresh, but she had a sharp nose and her manner was reserved. Prince William Henry told Lord Hood that

she is a pretty and a sensible woman and may have a great deal of money if her uncle thinks proper. Poor Nelson is over head and ears in love. I frequently laugh at him about it. However, seriously, my Lord, he is in more need of a nurse than a wife. I do not really think he can live very long.

Legal worries, as well as recurrent bouts of malaria, were responsible for his poor health, but he was paying court to

Fanny with as much zeal as he was chasing American interlopers. In view of how badly he treated her later on, one is apt to
sympathize with Fanny from the start. She certainly had no
idea of the passionate fires burning in the frail frame of her
suitor. There must be some significance in the fact that they had
no children, though Nelson had a daughter by Lady Hamilton.
Josiah turned out to be a lazy, unattractive lout, yet it was on
him rather than on Nelson that Fanny lavished her affections.
Her case goes by default, because her husband kept few letters
from her, while plenty of his survive. All one can say is that she
proved a dutiful wife, never wealthy because the expected
money never came her way, never beautiful, never passionate.
To be married to a genius in love with his profession may be bad
enough, but to have the most beautiful woman of the age for a
rival meant that poor Fanny never had a chance. For the first
ten years of their married life they were as happy as mortals
may expect to be; after that she became 'Tom Tit', the despised
and rejected rival to Emma's lavish affections.

There is something wrong about Nelson's early letters to
Fanny. Admittedly, he was soon writing in his normal spontaneous style, but he opens his courtship with the stilted conventions of the day. In his first letter (in which he spells her
name wrong) he asserts that he sincerely loves her, 'and I think
my affection is not only founded upon the principles of reason
but also upon the basis of mutual attachment'. A fortnight
later he claims that 'my greatest wish is to be united to you; and
the foundations of all conjugal happiness, real love and esteem,
is, I trust, what you believe I possess in the strongest degree towards you'. Reporting the news of his engagement to his
brother, he says that 'every day I am more than ever convinced
of the propriety of my choice'.

The language is that of a suitor rather than a lover. They
were married at Nevis in 1787, Prince William Henry giving the
bride away. Lawsuits plagued their honeymoon, but Nelson told
Locker that at last he had found happiness 'I am married to an
amiable woman, that makes amends for everything : indeed, till
I married her I never knew happiness. And I am morally certain

she will continue to make me a happy man for the rest of my days'.

Soon afterwards his ship was ordered home, Fanny taking a passage in a merchantman. For the next five years they lived together on half-pay – eight shillings a day – for the sake of economy in the cold rooms of the rectory at Burnham Thorpe. It is not an interesting period of Nelson's life. He was bored and restless, the long East Anglian days only occasionally broken by Court levées or visits to the Admiralty to beg for a ship: 'If your Lordships should be pleased to appoint me to a cockle boat I shall feel grateful'. He was convinced that Hood had taken against him, though the truth was that there was not a ship to be had for such a junior captain.

Nothing stirred in the world outside the parochial life of a Norfolk village until the Bastille fell and France staggered into the Revolution which her bankruptcy after the American War precipitated. Such events were not noticed in the few letters which Nelson wrote at this time. His politics were not those of the young Wordsworth, so that he never felt that it was bliss to be alive at the time. What he wanted was to return to the sea, which he loved above everything.

In 1792 events moved faster. The King of France was imprisoned, the battle of Valmy won, the Low Countries invaded, the Scheldt closed to shipping and in January 1793, Louis XVI was executed. Britain's sentiments as well as her traditional vital interests were challenged, since war was inevitable as long as Antwerp remained pointed like a pistol at her heart. Before war was actually declared on 11 February, the Admiralty had taken the usual precautions.

'After clouds come sunshine', quoted Nelson, the fighting man. He was now thirty-four years old, restored in health and at the peak of his powers if opportunity were granted him. In January he was summoned to London. The First Lord promised him a third-rate and in the meantime gave him a fourth-rate, the *Agamemnon*, built at Buckler's Hard on the Beaulieu river. To Nelson she was 'without exception one of the finest sixty-fours in the service'. His orders were to join Hood in the Mediterranean as soon as she was ready to sail. 'I not only like the ship, but I think I am well appointed in officers, and we are manned exceedingly well; therefore, have no doubt we shall acquit ourselves well, should the French give us a meeting.'

Two months before he wrote that, all was not exceedingly well, because the ship was a hundred men short of her complement of 450. 'Men are very hard to get and without a press I have no idea that our fleet can be manned.' Every captain was saying the same thing. Nelson sent his own gangs through Norfolk, as well as enlisting enough volunteers from the villages near Burnham. Josiah was taken on board as a Captain's Servant, as was another boy who became one of the finest frigate captains of the age – William Hoste, the son of a neighbouring parson. As young Hoste told his father, 'Captain Nelson is acknowledged to be one of the first characters in the service, and is universally beloved by officers and men'. Under such auspices it was a case of 'To Glory we steer'.

3 The Mediterranean Fleet

The war between Britain and France which opened in 1793 continued, with one brief intermission, until 1815, ten years after Nelson's death. The first few years are distinguished by only one notable victory – Howe's defeat of the French fleet at the Glorious First of June. The true Nelsonian period, in which supremacy at sea was established for a hundred years, thus comprises the few years between 1797 and 1805, during which almost every year was marked by some brilliant success at sea. The turn of the Army came later.

The undistinguished character of the opening phase of the war was chiefly due to the strategic incompetence of Henry Dundas, to whom Pitt left the higher direction of military affairs and who must be regarded as the worst Secretary of War this country has ever suffered. Dundas fought an old-fashioned war to take advantage of the domestic broils prevailing in France in order to seize her overseas possessions. This entailed sending small bodies of troops to all parts of the world, as well as making feeble attempts to land on the continent of Europe, from which the Army was always rapidly and ignominiously expelled. The price in the lives of soldiers of the regular army who perished in their thousands of tropical and other diseases may be illustrated by the fact that the seizure (and then the loss) of the unimportant island of St Lucia cost as many casualties as the whole of the Peninsular War.

Another aspect of this policy, supported by Burke, who regarded the war as an ideological conflict, was the support given to Royalist opposition from the sea at such points as La Vendée and Toulon. It was to implement this policy that

Hood's fleet was ordered to seize the latter, until it was retaken soon afterwards by an unknown captain of artillery named Bonaparte. To support such partisan uprisings proved then, as it has often proved since, a difficult and unrewarding operation.

The names of Napoleon and Nelson symbolize the new type of warfare which was in process of developing. After the French Revolution began to expand beyond its frontiers, wars could no longer be regarded as the 'temperate and undecisive contests' of Gibbon's day. They were no longer the sport of kings, fought by small professional armies and navies for limited objectives and conducted according to the rigid conventions prevailing in the eighteenth century. The conduct of war became total, to be fought by enormous conscript armies, wars between peoples and ideas. To Burke, the war was fought against 'an armed principle'. To Nelson, it was more simply a conflict against France herself. War, said Clausewitz afterwards, 'suddenly became an affair of the people', to be perfected by Bonaparte as 'a military power, based on the strength of the whole nation, [which] marched over Europe, smashing everything in pieces'. Napoleon inherited the revolutionary fervour of a nation in arms, but he was no tactical innovator. His genius lay in his ability to manoeuvre great bodies of troops to achieve rapid and surprising concentrations of force. God, he said, was on the side of the big battalions, a dictum which Nelson expressed in more conventional language when he said that only numbers could annihilate. For both of them the object was the same: total victory, not a limited war of positions or diplomatic gambits.

On neither side did new weapons play an important part in these developments. As far as the Royal Navy was concerned, only one useful new weapon had recently been introduced – the murderous, short-range carronade carried on the upper deck. The new inventions made at this time which pointed to the future – the rocket, the shell using Shrapnel's shot, the torpedo – were too feeble and unreliable in their infancy to make any difference to warfare as yet. Nelson himself was satisfied with the means at his disposal, provided that they were properly used, that is to say the line-of-battle ship armed with muzzle-loading guns firing solid shot with a short range. 'I shall of course look at it,' he told a correspondent who suggested a new type of gun-sight, 'but I hope we shall be able, as usual, to get so close to our enemies that our shot cannot miss their object.'

In his view, everything depended on training and tactics. His gun crews must be so regularly exercised that their rate of fire could be reckoned as three rounds in two minutes, with an effective range of not much more than half a kilometre (quarter of a mile). His officers must be sufficiently seamanlike to manoeuvre their ships rather than their guns so as to bring a full broadside to bear. They must be enterprising enough to cap-ture ships by boarding rather than by sinking, since solid shot was incapable of sinking wooden ships unless an accidental ex-plosion occurred (as happened at the battle of the Nile), or unless enemy ships were so damaged that they were run on shore (as at Trafalgar).

He was the greatest tactical genius of the age of sail because he was able to break the conventional sanctity of the Line of Battle. Fortunately, his early service in frigates, which were normally used in the role of cruisers or scouts, debarred him from being conditioned by the line-of-battle mentality. He never shared the view prevalent earlier in the century that 'a line of battle is the basis and formulation of all discipline in sea fights'. Rodney had shown at the battle of the Saints in 1782 the rich reward which followed breaking the enemy's line. Unless this was done, or unless a general chase in which individual captains could choose their opponents was ordered (as at Hawke's victory at Quiberon Bay), it was impossible to reach a decision, if num-bers were equally matched. French tactical authorities were satisfied with the way in which fleets of equal strength could be manoeuvred like a *corps de ballet*, and could boast that 'there are no longer decisive battles at sea, that is to say battles on which the end of the war absolutely depends'. Nelson was to change all that.

Apart from his natural offensive spirit, two factors operated in his favour. One was the new method of signalling introduced by Howe and Kempenfelt in 1782, and extended by Sir Home

Popham's *Marine Vocabulary* of 1800. By using flags to denote numbers referring to a dictionary of words, an admiral could explain more clearly what he wanted done, instead of relying on the few ambiguous orders contained in the antiquated code known as the Fighting Instructions. The other factor was the state of the enemy fleets which he encountered. Their lack of experience at sea and, generally speaking, their low professional morale enabled him to take risks which would have been impossible against the well-trained navy of pre-revolutionary days.

When war broke out, the Royal Navy consisted of some 400 warships, 115 of them ships of the line. The French navy consisted of 250, and of the 76 ships of the line only 27 were in commission. During the early years of the Revolution the officer corps, riddled with class distinctions, had been swept away. Half of their number emigrated or were disgraced, so that when it came to building a new republican navy the task was made all the more difficult. The Jacobins found the ports in ruins and when the fleets dared to put to sea discipline was chaotic. This state of affairs was remedied with astonishing speed, but even when officers of the *ancien régime* were reinstated – men like Nelson's opponents Brueys, Villeneuve, Ganteaume or Decrès, Napoleon's ineffective Minister of Marine – the thread of continuity had been broken and the British blockading fleets prevented them from gaining experience at sea.

British sea power, on the other hand, was firmly based on a large and efficient fleet in which most of the officers had been trained in a war which had only ended ten years previously. There was a flourishing merchant marine to provide a pool of seamen to man the fleet and to maintain the sinews of war. And there were overseas bases to serve as springboards for amphibious attacks on French possessions overseas. The instrument was there: it only needed the leadership which Nelson provided, and the strategic insight of admirals like his master, St Vincent, to lead it to victory.

At home, the administrative framework might be corrupt and cumbersome, but Lord Barham was the best of Comptrollers (far superior, in fact, to his predecessor, Nelson's uncle) and a succession of remarkable Secretaries – Nepean, Marsden, Croker and Barrow – made the machine work. Since in those days communications were so slow (it took six weeks for orders to reach the Mediterranean), all depended on the calibre and the initiative of the commander on the spot. It was a situation which exactly suited an individualist like Nelson.

Whether or not he was a great strategist is a matter for argument, but he was certainly a tactician of genius, combining in a supreme degree the virtues of patriotism, zeal, imagination and daring. Because he was a man who never suffered from the universal human failing of fear, he could take calculated risks which no ordinary commander could consider. He was adept in communicating his ideas and his enthusiasm to his subordinates, and by his personal example as well as the care which he took about their welfare, he could inspire his men to feats which seemed beyond their capabilities.

On 27 May 1793 Lord Hood's fleet of fifteen ships sailed from Gibraltar for the blockade of Toulon. Compared with the three-decker flagship *Victory*, Nelson's *Agamemnon* was one of the smaller ships, but she was also one of the best sailers and therefore suitable for the various diplomatic missions he was to be sent on during the coming months.

Apart from an ingrained antipathy to the French, he does not seem to have been aware as yet of the wider implications of the war. Like so many in England, he was confident that it would soon be over. Nor was he sure what it was all about, or that it was to be fought on a European scale. Hood's movements were part of the contribution made by Britain to the First Coalition, in which Austria, Prussia, Spain, Piedmont and Naples were already engaged. French troops had so far repulsed it by overrunning the Low Countries and pushing the invaders back across the Rhine. A thrust towards Italy (then dominated by Austria) was inevitable now that Revolutionary armies were spilling forward over the traditional frontiers of France.

Internally, however, the Republic was on the brink of civil war. In Marseilles and Toulon the Royalists had taken over, so that after a few months of blockade the dominant faction raised

the white flag of the Bourbons at Toulon and the leading citizens
came on board the flagship to surrender the city, together with a
fleet of twenty-one ships of the line which lay in the harbour.
Nelson imagined that this astonishing piece of good fortune was
due to the stringency of the blockade, but it was in fact dictated
entirely by domestic politics.

The surrender of the port placed Hood and General David
Dundas, commanding the 2,000 British troops on board, in a
difficult position because they were not sufficient to hold the
city. Nelson was therefore sent to the court of Naples to obtain
another 10,000. Some 3,000 ultimately arrived, together with
contingents from Spain, Piedmont and of course the Royalist
citizens, but with such a motley force it was only a matter of
time before the Jacobins counter-attacked from the north.

Nelson had no part in all this because he was constantly
absent on diplomatic missions to Genoa, Tunis, Leghorn and
Corsica, as well as Naples. In five months he reckoned that his
ship was at anchor for only twenty days. It was not the sort of
war which he had envisaged: there was no tangible enemy, no
prizes – 'all we get is honour and salt beef'. Nevertheless a wider
world was opening to him in which he showed himself as good
a diplomatist as he was a naval officer.

The residence of the British plenipotentiary at Naples,
decorated by Robert Adam, was not the sort of house he had
ever entered before. Old Sir William Hamilton he must have
known by reputation as the most distinguished archaeologist
of the age, a famous collector of vases and statuary and the
patron of the excavations at Pompeii and Herculaneum. The
two men had nothing in common, but Nelson was welcomed
with warm hospitality and introduced to the young Lady Hamilton. At this time he probably knew little of Emma's extraordinary history, though he could not fail to be impressed by her
looks. All that he told his wife about this first, brief meeting was
that she 'has been wonderfully kind and good to Josiah. She is a
young woman of aimiable manners, who does honour to the
station to which she is raised'. According to Sir William, she was
'better than anything in the antique', because her famous 'atti-

tudes' brought to life his collection of Greek vases, now in the British Museum. Emma's account of that first meeting, with which she fed her chosen biographer of Nelson twenty-five years later, was of course more dramatic. According to her, Sir William told her that she was going to meet 'a little man who could not boast of being very handsome, but who would become the greatest man that England ever produced'. It is most unlikely that he ever made such a remark at that date.

Nelson was at Leghorn when Toulon fell on 19 December. The key to the fighting over the past few weeks had been the appearance of a twenty-three year old lieutenant of artillery, Napoleon Bonaparte, as he then called himself, who sited Republican batteries with such skill that he made the harbour untenable. Before evacuating the town, Hood determined to destroy the arsenal and the fifty-eight ships of various sizes in the harbour, a task which he unwisely deputed to the undisciplined Spaniards and to an importunate young captain named Sir Sidney Smith, who had recently arrived from the eastern Mediterranean and had asked for the job. Nelson was later to have a violent quarrel with this arrogant but well-connected officer who, on the present occasion, badly bungled his duty. The arsenal, dock buildings and magazines were certainly blown up. Fourteen ships were burned, nine others towed out to sea, but twenty-five were left undamaged because of the haste in which things were done under a hail of enemy fire. Among the ships taken out were the *Minerve* frigate, which Nelson was to command for a time, and the *Commerce de Marseille*, the biggest ship in the world of 2,747 tons. She and the Spanish *Santissima Trinidada* (which Nelson was to encounter in two of his battles) were the only four-deckers afloat, compared with which the three-decker *Victory* was nothing in size or strength, but when she was brought back to England her hull was found to be in such poor condition that she was taken to pieces.

Nelson saw enough of the aftermath of the evacuation (as did Napoleon) never to forget it. Some 15,000 Royalist refugees were taken on board British ships to be escorted to Leghorn, while 200 executions a day were perpetrated by the Jacobins in another reign of terror. As he told his father, the scene of horror might be imagined but could not be described.

Some other base was now required if operations were to continue in the Gulf of Lions. Corsica was the obvious choice, especially as Boswell's General Paoli offered the island to Britain if she would help him get rid of the French. The harbour of San Fiorenzo was occupied without difficulty, but the capture of the larger town of Bastia, twenty kilometres (twelve miles) away, presented greater difficulties. The task was not made easier when one of those quarrels between the high command of the Army and the Navy, which had ruined so many combined operations in the past, broke out.

To understand this discreditable affair, in which, needless to say, Nelson was a violent though junior partisan, it must be remembered that Hood was now a man of seventy, twice the age of his protagonist. His record in the last war, when he quarrelled with senior officers like Rodney and Graves, showed how uncooperative he could be. Nelson may have regarded him as the greatest sea officer he knew, but that was before he met St Vincent. In peace time, as we have seen, relations had cooled between them, but before the end of the Corsican adventure Hood's feelings towards his zealous young colleague had warmed to genuine friendship.

General David Dundas (later Commander-in-Chief of the British Army) had nothing to compare with Hood's record in war, owing his appointment to the fact that he was brother of the Secretary of War. Hood had not been impressed with his conduct at Toulon, so that the traditional hostility between the services flared up when the general flatly refused to move against Bastia. 'In answer to which,' Hood wrote in his most arrogant style, 'I must take the liberty to observe that, however visionary and rash an attempt to reduce Bastia may be in your opinion, to me it appears very much the reverse, and to be a perfectly right measure.' Under the circumstances, he added the next day, 'I do not hesitate to say that your power [as commander-in-chief] ceased after the evacuation of Toulon, when the troops as well as the ships were at my disposal'. In a letter incoherent with rage, Dundas demanded to see the authority by which Hood claimed to command the troops. He then read the whole correspondence to his staff, sent in his resignation and retired to England.

Behind the principals in this quarrel were younger officers who were to become far more famous. Colonel John Moore, of Corunna fame, and Captain Horatio Nelson. They naturally took the sides of their respective commanders, Moore writing in his diary that 'We all agreed as to the absurdity of Lord Hood's pretensions to command the land force, and agreed to resist any such attempt'; while Nelson supported Hood when the latter said that 'the General's faculties seem to be palsied – we must therefore do the best we can'.

What lay at the root of the trouble was the unresolved question of the chain of command, hence the burden of responsibility and decision, in an operation involving both seamen landed from boats and troops attacking on shore. Throughout the history of combined operations this has been a fertile cause of disagreement. Are marines to be regarded as soldiers or sailors? At what point does the responsibility of an admiral give way to that of a general? Who, in fact, commands?

Fortunately, Nelson got on better with the artillery commander on the spot, as he busied himself with landing seamen to haul the guns into position. Throughout the siege, during which he spent eight weeks ashore, he virtually commanded the 12,000 troops and 300 seamen involved, while Moore sulked in his tent. As Dundas's temporary successor was a nonentity ('It is difficult to speak more nonsense than he does with more gravity and decorum', as Moore put it), Nelson remained the active liaison between the two services; and since he regarded any failure to attack as a national disgrace, he threw himself heart and soul into the siege. A stream of short, hasty letters gives evidence of his frienzied activity.

The place surrendered on 22 May. Next day General Stuart (a much under-rated commander who died too early to achieve fame) arrived to take over. Relations with Hood improved immediately. Moore's comment after the town surrendered is not only ungracious but fatuous, 'The land attack made by Lord Hood, though he will gain credit for it at home, was absurd to a degree. He never advanced one inch. The distance of his post, together with the unaccountable want of enterprise in the enemy, saved his troops from destruction.'

All the more credit to Nelson, who was responsible for the whole conduct of operations. But this is exactly what he did not receive in Hood's despatch, a lack of recognition of his services which wounded him deeply in spite of the fact that Hood was writing to him privately in the warmest terms. In letters to his own friends Nelson recapitulates all that he had done ('I was the mover of it – I was the cause of its success', etc.) and complains that while everyone else 'has got some place or other, I, only I, am without reward'.

To complete the reduction of Corsica it was necessary to follow up the success at Bastia with the capture of Calvi, a smaller town on the other side of the island which was defended by immense bastions, a *place forte* if ever there was one. Nelson entered into the attack with his usual indefatigable zeal, in spite of bouts of malaria, and on this occasion the army under Stuart proved much more cooperative. Moreover, he had the satisfaction of having as his right-hand man a naval captain who was a veritable St Peter in the band of his disciples – Ben Hallowell, a giant of a man who was a tower of strength in his later victories.

Calvi capitulated on 10 August. The siege is chiefly notable as the occasion of Nelson's first major wound. On 12 July, when manning a battery near the bastion, an enemy shot fell close to him, casting up a shower of stones and sand. 'My right eye is cut entirely down', he wrote four days later, though to his wife this was toned down to 'the blemish is nothing; not to be perceived, unless told.' But he could only distinguish between light and darkness and the surgeons told him that he would never recover the sight of that eye. Hence the 'very slight scratch' became officially reckoned for the purpose of compensation to be 'full equal to the loss of an eye'. No one knows the exact nature of the wound, but it was probably a lesion of the retina.

Most people imagine that thereafter Nelson wore a patch

over his right eye. Such was not the case, nor is he ever depicted as wearing one in contemporary portraits. Six years later he showed the wound to Dr Thomas Trotter, senior Physician of the Fleet, who found 'a membraneous substance seemingly spreading fast over the pupil'. Trotter recommended bathing it with cold water and wearing a green shade to protect both eyes against the glare at sea. Such a shade, like the peak of a cap, is attached to the tricorn hat preserved with his effigy at Westminster Abbey. On the authority of Dr Beatty, who attended him at Trafalgar, it used to be thought that he would have gone blind in both eyes on account of the strain to the left eye, but this is regarded today as probably incorrect.

After the fall of Calvi, Hood returned home, leaving the command of the fleet to Vice-Admiral Hotham. The latter's easy-going ways irked a man of Nelson's temperament, so that the next few months found him impatient and unsatisfied with the progress of events. A brush with the Toulon fleet off Genoa illustrates the contrasting characters of the two men. Nelson wrote to his wife when his first fleet action seemed imminent:

A glorious death is a debt to be envied; and if anything happens to me, recollect that death is a debt we must all pay, and whether now, or a few years hence, can be of little consequence. God bless you, and believe me ever your most faithful and affectionate husband.

When the two fleets of almost equal strength sighted each other on 13 March 1796, Nelson hoped for action, but the French bore away and Hotham was left satisfied that the threat to Corsica had been removed. The next day, however, the 84-gun *Ça Ira* collided with another ship and dropped astern after losing her topmasts. Nelson in the van saw an opportunity not to be missed, because his *Agamemnon* was such a fast sailer. The fact that the enemy was a much bigger ship, and that there was no sign of any other ship supporting him except Captain Fremantle in a frigate, did not deter him. He double-shotted his guns and when within a hundred yards of the enemy gave her a full broadside.

Scarcely a shot appeared to miss. The instant all were fired, we braced up our after yards, put the helm a-port, and stood for her again. This manoeuvre we practised till one p.m., never allowing the *Ça Ira* to get in single gun from either side to fire on us. They attempted some of their after-guns, but all went far ahead of us. At this time the *Ça Ira* was a perfect wreck, her sails hanging in tatters, mizen topmast and cross jack yards away.

The arrival of a second big French ship to tow her away forced him to break off action, but next day both ships surrendered. Thereupon he hastened on board the flagship to persuade Hotham to allow a general chase of the remainder, though the wind was light. 'But he, much cooler than myself, said "We must be contented, we have done very well".' So ended 'the miserable action' of 13 March.

The limitations of sea power as exercised with the restraint which Hotham approved became apparent during the next twelve months. It was obvious that the French army would move into Nice, then Piedmontese territory, and thence along the coast road skirting the Alps towards the Republic of Genoa. Northern Italy was then dominated by the antique Austrian army, and once that army was defeated in the field the whole plain of Lombardy with the territories of Mantua and Tuscany, even the Republic of Venice, would fall into French hands. In later years Nelson expressed the opinion that the British fleet might have prevented the invasion of Italy if it had been kept on the Riviera. This is more than doubtful, unless a landing in force were made to cut the coastal road and the Toulon fleet were destroyed. Hotham was incapable of doing the latter and there was no disposable force for the former.

Under such circumstance all that could be done was to send the *Agamemnon* with a flotilla of frigates and sloops to interrupt communications by sea. It could not be called a real blockade, because fast little tartanes, polacres and xebecs from Genoa or Leghorn were not to be deterred from selling their cargoes of corn by a handful of cruisers. The situation must have reminded Nelson of his experience in the West Indies. There were too many neutrals and too many small fast vessels engaged in the traffic for him to stop them all, and as before he realized that his admiral would never support him if he got into a scrape with the law. There was little honour in such duty and not much reward. His prize accounts for the three years he was in the Mediterranean show that he only received £2,226 for the whole period, of which his share in the *Ça Ira* amounted to £600.

But he was given plenty of experience as a diplomatist. The more he studied the European scene, the more depressed he became. The First Coalition against Revolutionary France was fast collapsing and when the push came it was clear to him that the whole political structure of Italy would disintegrate. Spain was the first to defect by signing a separate peace treaty. Closer acquaintance with the Austrian army on the coast convinced him 'by ocular demonstration, of the futility of Continental Alliances': not only would it be defeated at the first blow, but the court of Vienna would willingly come to terms. Tuscany and Naples would follow suit and all Italy would be overrun. 'Holland and Flanders they have entirely stripped; Italy is the gold mine, and, if once entered, is without the means of resistance.'

He hoped that Hood would return to put some vigour into their operations, but Hood's egoism had led to a final breach with the Admiralty when the latter refused his request for more ships, without which he said that 'he could not consider his professional character safe'. Instead, there appeared in November Sir John Jervis, aged sixty-three, a self-made man and a thorough professional.

The two men had never met before, so that at first their relations were strictly formal. It was not long before Jervis, a keen judge of character, realized that in the captain of the *Agamemnon* he had an officer after his own heart. At the same time Nelson became aware of the integrity and professional competence behind the gruff exterior and the positively sadistic insistence on strict discipline for which the old man was notorious. Jervis, far more than Hood, was his master, so that it is almost literally true that it was Jervis who flogged into shape the fleets which Nelson led to victory.

Though no opportunity of showing the worth of the fleet

was vouchsafed that winter, Nelson was rewarded for his zeal by the confidence which Jervis placed in him. 'The admiral,' Nelson told Fanny, 'seems to consider me more as an associate than a subordinate officer.' 'There is nothing within my grasp', the admiral told him, 'that I shall not be proud to confer on you.' This meant the broad pennant of a commodore, which was a post and not a rank, as it still is. When the *Agamemnon* after three years at sea without a refit was obviously nothing more than a hulk, she was sent home and Nelson was transferred to the seventy-four-gun *Captain*. The captain of this bigger ship was an American Loyalist named Ralph Miller, born at New York but serving with great distinction throughout his life in the Royal Navy. Nelson was to owe much to him in his first big success at the battle of St Vincent.

Nelson became a Commodore on the same day as Napoleon issued his first Order of the Day to the Army of Italy on 27 March 1796. That famous order repeats in more grandiloquent terms what Nelson had been saying in his letters home :

Soldiers! you are naked and starving. The Government owes you much, but can do nothing for you. I will lead you into the most fertile plains in the world, where you shall find great towns, rich provinces – within your grasp, Glory, Honour, Riches! Soldiers of Italy! shall you be found wanting in constancy or courage?

The First Italian Campaign proved Bonaparte to be the greatest military genius of the age. It was a triumph of leadership to take that starving, shoeless rabble against the largest conventional army in Europe and to defeat it in a series of lightning operations. As Nelson foretold, the Austrians ran at the first shot, only to be out-manoeuvred again and again. By the time the French reached Milan, the Republic of Genoa and the Duchy of Tuscany had made peace. They were followed by the Kingdom of the Two Sicilies and ultimately by the Republic of Venice. Long before the Treaty of Campo Formio brought that brilliant campaign to a close, Spain had declared war against England and Jervis had received orders to evacuate Corsica and leave the Mediterranean. By the end of the year 1796 Britain was at the nadir of her fortunes. As Nelson had prophesied to his wife: 'England will soon carry on the war alone and, instead of having all Europe in our alliance and pay, we shall have them in a certain degree all against us.'

4 St Vincent

The year 1796 ended with the British evacuating the Mediterranean and the French fleet from Brest transporting troops for
the invasion of Ireland, then in a state of rebellion. The descent
on Bantry Bay, led by General Hoche to rival Bonaparte's suc-
cesses in Italy, and by Wolfe Tone the Irish patriot, might well
have succeeded, because only one British ship ever sighted the
huge armament either on its way out or on its way back. It
failed by the accident of a snowstorm on Christmas Day, so that
not a man was landed nor a shot fired. But the ease with which
the vigilance of the Channel Fleet had been evaded encouraged
plans for a further attempt – this time from Holland. That, too,
was defeated towards the end of the year. Had such an attempt
been made during the summer, when nearly every ship in a
home port was in a state of mutiny, it might well have been a
different story; but the French were not ready, the chance was
lost, and the mutineers returned to their allegiance to fight magnificently under Duncan at the battle of Camperdown.

The mutiny was really a strike over the abominable conditions prevailing at sea. It was provoked by the inactivity of the
Channel Fleet under Lord Bridport and it was badly mishandled
by the Admiralty. The Mediterranean Fleet, on the other hand,
was under the command of one of the strictest disciplinarians
who ever lived, an admiral who kept his ships constantly on the
alert, with a keen eye on the behaviour of both officers and men.
Sir John Jervis had spent a year training his fleet to an extraordinary degree of efficiency. 'At home they know not what this
fleet is capable of performing, any and everything', Nelson told
his wife. 'Of all the fleets I ever saw, I never saw one in point of

officers and men to our present one, and with a commander-in-chief fit to lead them to glory.' After two major victories had proved his point, he wrote no more than the truth when he told the old admiral that 'We look to you, as we have always found you, as to our Father, under whose fostering care we have been led to fame'.

There were many who disliked the methods by which such care was manifested. Jervis was as much the enemy of 'gimcrack and frippery' among officers as he was of slackness or indiscipline among their men. Mutineers were hanged at the yard arm on a Sunday morning to impress the fleet, and any officer found guilty of dereliction of duty soon found himself on the way home. Though critical of the way Pitt was running the war, no man ever had a higher sense of duty than Jervis whom the King liked to refer to as 'my old oak'. All through the months spent blockading Toulon, he constantly exercised the fleet in evolutions and manoeuvres, in station keeping and the exercise of the great guns and small arms. The easy routine of Hotham was forgotten in the state of activity in which Jervis kept his ships on close blockade. As he wrote with stern pride to the First Lord,

We have no relaxation in port, where we never go without positive necessity; the officers are all kept to their duty; no sleeping on shore, or rambling about the country; and when at sea we do not make snug for the night, as in the Western Squadron [the Channel Fleet] but are working incessantly by the lead to keep our position, insomuch as both mind and body are continually upon the stretch.

For twelve months he bombarded the Navy Board with complaints about the shortage of planks, lead, twine, masts, yards, canvas, and no one could write a ruder letter to those responsible for sending him ships which were 'a complete sieve from the poop to the orlop deck'. Equally at fault were the Commissioners of Sick and Wounded so that it is significant that soap, the best antidote to typhus or ship fever, and lemon juice, the proved prophylactic against scurvy, were first officially issued in his fleet. Consequently, as Nelson said, 'You taught us to keep seamen healthy without going into port, and to stay at sea for years without a refiit.'

All this would have been of small avail had Jervis not had the good fortune to command a remarkable set of sea officers, later to be called by Nelson his Band of Brothers. Nelson was but the first among equals, though Jervis deserves the credit for discerning his genius and providing opportunities for its exercise. Collingwood was now in the Mediterranean, and we have already met stalwart fighters such as the Canadian-born Hallowell and the American Loyalist Miller. The officer whom Jervis regarded as the finest of them all was Thomas Troubridge, to whom he paid the noble compliment that he possessed 'honour and courage bright as his sword'. On occasion he might question Nelson's impetuosity; he never doubted Troubridge's capability, so that when the latter was drowned he was heard to mutter, 'I shall never see Troubridge's like again. I loved that invaluable man.'

Edward Berry, Nelson's first lieutenant in the *Agamemnon*, followed him to the *Captain*. At the age of twenty-eight he still looked like a boy on account of his fair complexion. Nelson got him promoted captain because 'he is a protégé of mine and I know him to be an officer of talents, great courage and laudable ambition'. Like many of the others, he was the son of a tradesman, as Jervis was the son of a civil servant and Nelson that of a parson. This was an essentially middle-class group, who had to depend on their own efforts because they possessed no influence to help them forward in their careers.

One of the chief mourners at Nelson's funeral, Lord Radstock, was now Vice-Admiral Waldegrave. In his capacity of captain of the *Barfleur* he represented the virtues of the aristocracy, just as Sir Charles Knowles did its vices – 'an imbecile', according to Jervis, 'totally incompetent and the *Goliath* of no use whatsoever under his command'. Yet it was this ship under the command of Thomas Foley (now captain of the *Britannia*) which was to be the leading ship at the Nile, and it was Foley whom Nelson intended to be captain of his fleet at Trafalgar. He was replaced on account of ill health by Thomas Masterman

Hardy, who attended Nelson's last moments. Hardy was now a lieutenant, a big, serene fellow, blunt of speech and uncommonly dull on paper, but 'very superior, the very soul of truth'. His devotion to Nelson was doglike, not only on account of his admiration of him as a sea officer and the affection Nelson invariably inspired among those nearest to him, but because Nelson had saved his life.

The occasion nearly made Nelson miss his first big fleet action. When Jervis brought the fleet back to Lisbon, Nelson was sent to take off officials left on the island of Elba, the last of the British possessions in the Mediterranean. He was given two large frigates for the mission – *La Minerve*, a fine 38-gun vessel taken at Toulon, and the 32-gun *Blanche*. On his way east he sighted two Spanish frigates guarding the enemy fleet at Cartagena. The captain of the larger one was Don Jacobo Stuart, a lineal descendant of James II. As the *Minerve* ranged alongside the following dialogue took place:

'This is an English frigate. If you do not surrender, I will fire.'
'This is a Spanish frigate, and you may begin as soon as you please.'

The ships were exactly equal in size, so that the ensuing action was the sharpest Nelson had yet seen.

I asked him to surrender several times during the action, but his answer was 'No, sir, not whilst I have the means of fighting left.' When only himself and his officers were left alive, he hailed and said he would fight no more, and begged that I would stop firing. The next frigate was the *Ceres* of 40 guns, who did not choose to fight much. Not a mast, yard or rope but is hacked to pieces.

The loss of men was higher than in any single ship during the ensuing battle. Stuart was generously treated on board the *Minerve*, while lieutenants Culverhouse and Hardy were put on board the enemy ships to command the prize crews. However, a few hours later a number of Spanish ships moved out to sea. If he was to accomplish his mission, Nelson had no alternative but to abandon his captures with their prize crews still on board.

The *Minerve* proceeded to Elba, where the governor, Sir

Gilbert Elliot (later Lord Minto) and Colonel John Drinkwater were embarked. She returned to Gibraltar on 9 February 1797, where Nelson heard that the Spanish fleet had moved west to Algeciras. He only had time to effect an exchange of his prisoners for the two lieutenants left on board before hurrying off to warn Jervis that the enemy was on the way. The letter which he wrote to the Captain General of the province on that occasion is so typically courteous and humane that its conclusion is worth quoting:

I trust that these men, now prisoners of war with you, will be sent to Gibraltar. It becomes great nations to act with generosity to each other, and to soften the horrors of war.

I have the honour to be, with the most perfect esteem,
Your most obedient servant,
Horatio Nelson

As he was leaving the Bay of Algeciras, however, two large Spanish men-of-war gave chase. The frigate cleared for action but depended more on her sailing qualities to evade pursuit. Leaving her in the hands of her captain, Nelson and the newly-released Hardy went below. They had no sooner sat down to dinner than there was a cry of 'Man overboard'. The officers ran up on deck, the jolly boat was lowered and Hardy jumped in. But a strong current was running through the Gut, so that they were quickly carried towards the Spanish ships. Too late to save the drowning man, Nelson cried out 'By God, I'll not lose Hardy! Back the main topsail!'

The frigate's way was checked. The boat crew pulled harder against the current as the bulk of their pursuers loomed larger. But the Spanish captains, knowing that Nelson was on board, shortened sail and during the precious moments of delay Hardy was hauled on board again. Studding sails were spread and the *Minerve* began to draw away from her pursuers. By nightfall they were out of sight.

The rendezvous with the fleet was off Cape St Vincent, where Jervis moved it from Lisbon after a report that the Brest fleet might be coming south, whereas it actually went west to

Bantry Bay. After he heard about that fiasco he continued to cruise in the area because Villeneuve had already passed the straits in a gale with five ships and there was every prospect that the Spanish fleet might do the same. The Cape was the most likely place to intercept it, the number of actions fought there-abouts illustrating its importance in naval strategy as the junction between the Mediterranean and the Atlantic oceans. Cape Trafalgar lay a hundred and fifty kilometres (a hundred miles) south-east, and even today the Americans have chosen Rota in Cadiz Bay a few kilometres to the north as the site of their largest base in Europe.

Considerable resolution was required to face the numerically superior Spanish fleet, consisting as it did of the only four-decker afloat, the *Santissima Trinidada*, of 136 guns, six three-deckers of 112 guns, two two-deckers, the total being twenty-seven line-of-battle ships and eight frigates. What Jervis did not know was that there had been difficulties about selecting the commander-in-chief, and that when the fleet left Cartagena in compliance with French pressure it was exceedingly badly manned. On several occasions during the ensuing battle British seamen, peering into enemy gunports, saw crews quitting their stations as soon as the guns were run out. After Nelson captured the *San Josef* many tompions were found still fitted to the muzzles of guns which no one had attempted to fire. One of the reasons for the enormous risks he took was the low opinion he had formed of the Spanish navy when he first encountered it six years previously: 'The Dons may make fine ships,' he then wrote, 'they cannot, however, make men.'

Though the French government would have liked to see the Spanish fleet at Brest, Admiral Juan de Cordoba had his own reasons for bringing it round from Cartagena to Cadiz. He was not seeking action because his aim (of which Jervis was ignorant) was to escort a convoy of four large merchant vessels called *urcas* with a valuable cargo of mercury from the mines north of Málaga. Large supplies of this ore were necessary for amalgamating with the silver brought from the New World. This group, with its armed escort, was separated by a wide gap from the main body. Had Jervis known what was in the ships composing what he called 'the leeward division' of the enemy fleet, he might have paid more attention to it and the story, especially after the battle was fought, might have been different. As it was, he concentrated on the main body which composed what he called 'the weather division', so that the convoy escaped unscathed.

The valuable nature of the convoy explains why Cordoba was so anxious to join up with it. To effect this, he reversed the order of sailing, causing much confusion before battle was joined. Exactly the same thing happened before Trafalgar, where again this manoeuvre provided one of the principal reasons for Villeneuve's defeat on that occasion.

Though this tactical advantage was fully exploited on the day of battle, Jervis had been experiencing very considerable difficulties of his own during the previous weeks. Most of his ships had been at sea so long that their sailing qualities were affected. By a series of accidents, his modest numbers had been reduced, though there had been a welcome addition to his strength in the arrival of reinforcements under Rear-Admiral Sir William Parker – *Prince George, Namur, Orion, Irresistible, Colossus*. 'They are a valuable addition to my excellent stock,' he told the Admiralty, so that when the first news of the enemy's movements came in he assured their Lordships that 'I flatter myself we shall be able to deal with them.' Nevertheless, on the day of action he had only 15 ships (six of them three-deckers) and 4 frigates to oppose a force of 27 of the line and 8 frigates.

His advanced frigates gave him some warning of the approach of the enemy, but it was not until Nelson's arrival late on 13 February that he knew for certain how close they were. The Commodore had actually sailed right through them the previous night, when the *Minerve* seemed to be surrounded by huge shadowy shapes. The thick weather made it impossible to say if they were friend or foe. If morning light disclosed that the Spanish fleet lay between him and Jervis, Nelson decided to stretch away across to the West Indies, but at dawn the phantom fleet had disappeared.

Having given his news and transferred his passengers to the *Victory*, Nelson was piped aboard his own ship, the 74-gun *Captain*, to await the dawn of 14 February, St Valentine's Day. The commander-in-chief did not sleep that night. He sat up writing his will until the sound of the signal gun drew him from his cabin to the quarterdeck. All that he could see through the morning mist was the admirably close order which his ships had managed to preserve through the hours of darkness. He signalled his approbation, adding with a full realization of the political issues at stake: 'A victory is very essential to England at this moment.'

Troubridge led the line in the *Culloden*, with the *Victory* in the conventional position of a flagship in the centre. Nelson's *Captain* was the third ship from the rear, Collingwood's *Excellent* being the rearmost ship. The five frigates lay, as usual, outside the line of battle on the port quarter.

As the mist lifted, Cape St Vincent bearing thirty-nine kilometres (twenty-four miles) N E, Jervis could see that a gap had developed in the enemy fleet, the main body now lying several kilometres to windward. Robert Calder, captain of the fleet, reported the news to the admiral on the quarterdeck of the *Victory* as more ships came in sight.

'There are eight sail of the line, Sir John.'
'Very well, sir.'
'There are twenty sail of the line, Sir John.'
'Very well, sir.'
'There are twenty-five sail of the line, Sir John.'
'Very well, sir.'
'There are twenty-seven sail, Sir John.'
'Enough, sir, no more of that; the die is cast, and if there are fifty sail I will go through them.'

'That's right, Sir John!' exclaimed the gigantic Hallowell, slapping the admiral's back in his excitement, 'That's right, by God, we shall give them a damned good licking.'

The English line, steering a course S S W in order to pass through the gap, was formed at 11.29. In contrast to their close-

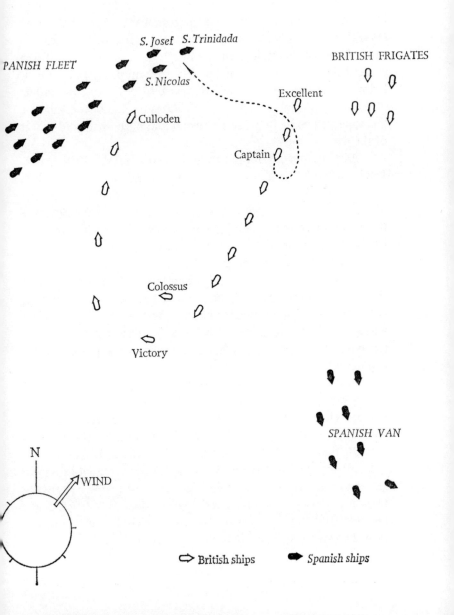

1300 hrs on 14 February 1797

The Battle of Cape St Vincent

SPANISH FLEET

S. Josef S. Trinidada

S. Nicolas

BRITISH FRIGATES

Excellent

Culloden

Captain

Colossus

Victory

SPANISH VAN

N

WIND

⇨ British ships   ➡ Spanish ships

hauled formation, Cordoba's ships fell off to leeward, some of them misunderstanding his intentions, so that the ships often lay three or four abreast in an ungainly bunch. When the *Culloden* opened fire at 12.08, Cordoba altered course in order that the *Santissima Trinidada* should lead the main body round the rear of the English fleet. The action became general from the British van to the centre as this happened, but the rear was unengaged. All the Spanish convoy division wore before the wind with the exception of one ship which tried to engage the *Victory*. A collision seemed imminent when the Spanish captain gave way, put his helm down and left himself exposed to a terrific broadside. 'Raked her both ahead and astern', states the log of the *Victory*, 'he appeared to be in great confusion and bore up, as did others of the enemy ships.'

As Cordoba attempted to pass astern of the British line, Jervis ordered his ships to tack in succession to follow him round. It was obvious to Nelson in the rear that by the time this manoeuvre was completed the Spaniards would have achieved their aim, because they had the advantage of the wind. In order to check them, he decided at one o'clock to wear his own ship out of the line to stand on the other tack himself and throw his ship at the leading Spanish ship. The log of the *Captain* states, 'The Commodore ordered the ship to be wore; when passing between the *Diadem* and *Excellent* [the two ships astern], she was immediately engaged with the S. *Trinidada* and two other three-decked ships, in which we were nobly supported by the *Culloden*.'

By throwing his two-decker across the path of the Spanish four-decker, which was supported by the three-deckers in her wake, Nelson forced them to alter course, thus giving time for the *Culloden*, *Blenheim* and others of the van to work their way into the main body. Only a tactician of genius and a man totally without fear would have dared to do this on his own initiative. Had he failed, had the *Captain* been dismasted before engaging, he would have been court-martialled for disobeying orders. But he knew his enemy and he intuitively assessed the risk of destruction. As Mahan well says in his account of the battle:

In this well-timed, but most daring move, which illustrates to the highest degree the immense difference between a desperate and a reckless action, Nelson passed to the head of the British column, crossing the bows of five large Spanish vessels, and with his 74 engaged the *Santissiama Trinidada* of 136 guns, the biggest ship at that time afloat.

The *Trinidada* was closely supported by the 112-gun *San Josef*, the 112-gun *Salvador del Mundo* and the 80-gun *San Nicolas*. The *Captain* herself was supported by Troubridge in the *Culloden*, who had fought his way up the Spanish column, and by Collingwood in the *Excellent* who had been told to follow his friend's example by wearing out of the line. 'It is a difficult thing for anyone, particularly one who is engaged, to relate the circumstances of a battle,' Collingwood wrote afterwards.

Everyone is so much employed by attention to his own situation and watching the movements and signals of the Admiral, that it is impossible to know exactly what others are doing. . . . After this we had neither order nor signals, for the Admiral was so satisfied with the impetuosity of the attack made by the ships ahead of him that he left us alone.

That was to be Nelson's way when he was in command. Now, as Collingwood told his wife, 'My good friend, the Commodore, had been long engaged, and I came happily to his relief, for he was dreadfully mauled.' For the next hour he engaged the *Trinidada*, trimming her so well, and forcing the *San Josef* to fall on board the *San Nicolas*, that Nelson could turn his attention to these ships. The *Captain*'s wheel was shot away, her foretopmast snapped by a chain shot and the whole ship so badly damaged that she could only continue to the fight by locking herself to one of the enemy.

Then followed an incident which caught the imagination of the nation. It was the sort of example of personal courage attended by unimaginable success which appealed to an age in which warfare still depended on the efforts of an individual. Nelson determined to board, and to lead the boarding party himself, though Berry was the first man to jump into the enemy's mizzen chains. Miller was about to do the same when Nelson held him back: 'No, Miller, I must have that honour.'

Supported by seamen carrying tomahawks and soldiers of the 69th (later Welch) Regiment, who were on board as marines, Nelson climbed up the stern of the *San Nicolas*. The story goes that, as he did so, he cried 'Westminster Abbey or Glorious Victory.'

A soldier having broken the upper quarter-gallery window, jumped in, followed by myself and others as fast as possible. I found the cabin door fastened, and some Spanish officers fired their pistols; but having broke open the doors, the soldiers fired, and the Spanish Brigadier or Commodore fell, as he was retreating to the quarter-deck near the wheel. Having pushed on to the quarterdeck, I found Captain Berry in possession of the poop, and the Spanish ensign hauling down. I passed with my people and Lieutenant Pierson on to the larboard gangway to the forecastle, where I met two or three Spanish officers, prisoners to my seamen, and they delivered me their swords. At this moment a fire of pistols or muskets open from the admiral's stern gallery of the *San Josef*. I directed the soldiers to fire into her stern; and calling to Captain Miller, ordered him to send more men into the *San Nicolas*, and directed my people to board the first-rate, which was done in an instant, Captain Berry assisting me into the main chains. At this moment a Spanish officer looked over from the quarterdeck rail and said they surrendered; from this most welcome intelligence it was not long before I was on the quarter-deck, where the Spanish Captain, with a bow, presented me his sword, and said the Admiral was dying of his wounds below. I asked him, on his honour, if the ship were surrendered? He declared she was; on which I gave him my hand and desired him to call his officers and ship's company to tell them of it, which he did; and on the quar-terdeck of a Spanish first-rate, extravagant as the story may seem, did I receive the swords of vanquished Spaniards; which, as I re-ceived, I gave to William Fearney, one of my bargemen, who put them with the greatest sangfroid under his arm.

Such was Nelson's Patent Bridge for Boarding First Rates, celebrated in scores of popular prints and paintings, and such was the way he first earned the plaudits of the people. The dramatic style of the episode overshadowed the hard fighting in the rear and even the battering given to the Spanish flagship throughout the afternoon. At one moment it was supposed that she had surrendered, but as the light faded on that short February day she staggered out of the mêlée before the wind in an attempt to rejoin the ships composing the convoy.

It was time to break off action and lie to for the night. The *Captain* was so badly damaged that she had to be towed away, while the five prizes, two of them Nelson's, had to be secured. Cordoba professed to interpret this as retirement, but neither side was in condition to continue the fight. He describes his own flagship as totally dismasted, incapable of making signals or hoisting lights. At a council of war the next morning it was agreed that action could not be renewed. When he ultimately reached Cadiz, he was arrested and sent to Madrid under an escort of cavalry.

The British fleet remained in good order, though so badly damaged that it was fortunate that it had not got to fight again. As the *Captain* was a floating wreck, Nelson transferred to the *Irresistible*, where he flew his flag as Rear-Admiral after having been promoted by seniority immediately after the battle.

Though the fighting had been hard and long, and an immense quantity of ammunition expended – 146 barrels of powder on board the *Captain*, 197 on board the *Prince George* – casualties only equalled those suffered in the ten-minute duel between the *Shannon* and the *Chesapeake* in the later Anglo-American war. One estimate puts the British total at 73 killed, 227 wounded, with 200 killed and 1,284 wounded on the Spanish side, in addition to 2,000 prisoners.

The consequences of the victory far outweighed such losses. Any attempt on the part of a Franco-Spanish fleet to invade the British Isles was now out of the question, and when such an attempt was made eight months later by a Dutch fleet it was defeated by Duncan in the much fiercer battle at Camperdown. The public rejoiced at such a victory after so many years of indecisive warfare. At Bath there were such celebrations that Nelson's old father felt himself 'obliged to retire from the public eye so that he might weep tears of joy in secret'.

But the grievances of the men composing the Channel Fleet were too deep to be forgotten in the flush of victory elsewhere, so that the great mutinies broke out at Spithead and the Nore two months later. One of the reasons why the trouble did not reach the Mediterranean fleet was undoubtedly the pride bred by the action of 14 February, just as one of the reasons for the greater victory at the Nile a year later was the confidence inspired on that day. What was undeniable was the appearance of a new star in the naval firmament and a new national hero, of which Britain stood in great need at that stage of the war. Nelson sailed into history at the battle of St Vincent.

His behaviour as soon as it was over made sure of that, for he was ever his best public relations officer. He rowed across to the flagship before even changing his uniform. The admiral received the battered little figure – part of his hat torn away, his coat split and his face stained with blood and powder – with open arms 'using every expression to make me happy'. Nor had he escaped unscathed. Though he referred to his bruises as trifling, he had in fact suffered an internal contusion which was to trouble him for the rest of his life. In spite of Jervis's unusual demonstration of affection, there were those who were jealous of the Commodore's contribution to the victory. Was it not, suggested Captain Calder, to say the least, unauthorized? 'It certainly was so,' snapped Jervis 'and if ever you commit such a breach of your orders I will forgive you also.'

The fact that there was so much to do, and that he was exhausted by the day's events explains the shortest letter Nelson ever wrote to his wife: 'I am well; Josiah is well.' To Collingwood he was more affectionate: 'My dearest friend – "A friend in need is a friend indeed" was never more truly verified than by your most noble and gallant conduct yesterday in sparing the *Captain* from further loss; and I beg, both as a public officer and a friend, you will accept my most sincere thanks. . . . Believe me, as ever, your most affectionate Horatio Nelson.' Collingwood's reply was equally generous: 'It added very much to the satisfaction I felt in thumping the Spaniards that I released you a little. The highest rewards are due to you and

Culloden: you formed the plan of attack, we were only accessories to the Don's ruin.'

Both men had suffered in the past – Collingwood after the First of June and Nelson after Corsica – from a grievance that their services had not been properly recognized in the public despatches. To be mentioned in despatches was a matter of real importance to ambitious officers, but commanders-in-chief were in the habit of describing their actions in general terms. If they began to mention names it meant breeding dissatisfaction by an invidious choice. Even on this occasion Jervis's despatch baldly states that 'confident in the skill, valour and discipline of the officers and men I had the happiness to command, and judging the honour of His Majesty's arms and the circumstances of the war in these seas, required a considerable degree of enterprise, I felt myself justified in departing from the regular system' – of tactics. This was, in fact, his second draft, Calder having advised him to suppress the first, because any eulogy of Nelson's conduct might encourage others to do the same without orders. The commander-in-chief therefore enclosed a personal letter with his public despatch commending various officers and stating that 'Commodore Nelson contributed very much to the fortunes of the day, as did Captain Collingwood'.

For his part, Nelson was taking no risks that his merits would be overlooked at home. He knew that Colonel Drinkwater and Sir George Elliot would be the first in London, so it was important to prime them. He took the trouble to row over to the frigate in which they were passengers. Elliot was not available, but Drinkwater was button-holed. Nelson received his congratulations 'with great modesty, though evidently with great satisfaction'. 'I'll tell you how it happened', continued Nelson, who thereupon dictated the whole story while Drinkwater took notes.

The conversation turned to rewards. The Admiral, thought Drinkwater, would of course be made a peer (he became Earl St Vincent), and 'as for you, Commodore, they will make you a baronet'. 'No, no if they want to mark my services, it must not be in that manner.' 'Oh,' said Drinkwater 'you wish to be made a Knight of the Bath?' 'Yes,' replied Nelson, 'if my services have been of any value, let them be noticed in a way that the public may know me, or them.' As foreseen, all this was passed on to Elliot and by him to the First Lord, with the result that the Order of the Bath was conferred on Nelson. For his coat of arms he chose as supporters a sailor holding the Broad Pennant of a Commodore and trampling on the Spanish flag, and a British lion. For his crest there was the stern of the *San Josef*, and for a motto 'Faith and Works'. He presented the sword which he took from the Spanish Rear-Admiral to the City of Norwich, which gave him its freedom; the sword is still preserved in the Guildhall.

His private correspondence displays a childish, though entirely justified glee in his own performance. For the Duke of Clarence he wrote a long self-congratulatory narrative; for his wife a somewhat laboured skit entitled 'Commodore Nelson's Receipt for an Olla Podrida, or Nelson's New Art of Cookery'. She, poor woman, merely begged him never to board again: 'Leave it to Captains.' The only discordant note was sounded by Sir William Parker, who took offence at the tone of the narrative when it was printed and sent the author a letter complaining that he had overlooked the gallantry and good conduct which marked every ship, especially his own and others in the rear: 'I feel much concern at the occasion of this letter, but remain etc., Parker.' For the public as a whole, and more particularly the seamen in the fleet, Nelson had taken the first step to achieve the sort of reputation which is commemorated on Hawke's tombstone by the noble words: 'Where'er he sailed, Victory attended him.'

But not quite yet. The battle was fought on 14 February. On 24 July he nearly lost his life. The battle had made him Rear-Admiral Sir Horatio Nelson K B, with the freedom of the cities of London and his native Norwich, but he had not yet achieved the ambition which he described to Fanny as that of 'having a gazette to myself: I feel that such an opportunity will be given me'. Being Nelson, he was ever seeking the chance to seize it.

For the next few months talk in the ships at Lisbon was naturally chiefly concerned with the extraordinary events which were taking place at Spithead and the Nore. It seemed unlikely that the mutiny would spread to Jervis's fleet, but no chances were being taken with the ships sent out to reinforce him. One of these, the *Theseus*, had been deeply implicated in the outbreak at home. She was placed under Nelson's command and it is surely significant that a fortnight later a scrap of paper was dropped on the quarterdeck:

Success attend Admiral Nelson! God bless Captain Miller! We thank them for the officers they have placed over us. We are happy and comfortable, and will shed every drop of blood in our veins to support them, and the name of the *Theseus* shall be immortalized as high as the *Captain's* – SHIP'S COMPANY.

The scheme for a punitive expedition against Spain which Nelson favoured was an attack on Santa Cruz, the harbour of Teneriffe used by returning silver fleets. It was the scene of Robert Blake's attack on the Spanish fleet at anchor in 1657, a fine precedent for the battle of the Nile, though 'I do not reckon myself equal to Blake'. What was now proposed was an amphibious attack to seize the town and castle, but the Army was not interested. It was therefore decided that a landing by seamen and marines should be made, covered by a bombardment from the ships – four 74s and three frigates. 'Under "General" Troubridge ashore and myself afloat, I am confident of success. Whenever I see the place, two hours shall decide its fate.'

The plan, carefully prepared as it was, displays all the marks of over-confidence. The result was a disaster, the worst in Nelson's career. A *coup de main* by Troubridge at the head of a thousand men failed because contrary currents prevented the boats approaching the shore before they were discovered. The alarm was given and Troubridge returned to the *Seahorse* to consult Nelson about the next step.

The captain of the frigate was Nelson's old friend Thomas Fremantle, who had fallen in love with Miss Betsey Wynne

when evacuating her family from Leghorn the previous year.
The progress of the affair is delightfully recorded in Betsey's
vivacious diary. After they were married she remained on board
to act as hostess to her friend Admiral Nelson.

It was decided to mount another attack on the night of 24
July: 'They are all [i.e. Troubridge and the marines, with
Nelson, Fremantle and Bowen in the boats] to land in the
town', wrote Betsey. 'As the taking of this place seemed an easy
and almost sure thing, I went to bed after they were gone, apprehending no danger for Fremantle.'

What actually happened was that Troubridge reached the
town square with his redcoats to await reinforcements from
the second wave of boats before attacking the citadel. No one
appeared. The boats carrying the seamen and scaling ladders
were wrecked by the surf at the landing place near the mole.
'Such a heavy fire of musketry and grape shot was kept on us
from the citadel and houses at the head of the mole that we
could not advance, and we were nearly all killed or wounded.'
Bowen was killed. Both Fremantle and Nelson were shot in the
right arm, Fremantle in the fleshy part, but Nelson's elbow was
shattered. He fell back into the arms of his stepson crying 'I am
shot through the arm. I am a dead man.' Whatever Josiah's faults,
he saved Nelson's life on that occasion, as Nelson acknowledged.
The artery having been severed, a tourniquet was made from the
silk handkerchief he wore round his neck. With cannon shot
passing over their heads, Josiah ordered the boat to pull back to
the ship. As they passed the *Fox* cutter she was hit between wind
and water and her whole crew of 97 men perished.

After a long pull, with Nelson lying at the bottom of the
boat only half conscious from loss of blood, they reached the
Seahorse. Nelson refused to go on board: 'I had rather suffer
death than alarm Mrs Fremantle by her seeing me in this state,
and when I can give her no tidings whatever of her husband.'
So they rowed on to the *Theseus*, where Midshipman Hoste saw
him hauled on board, clinging with one hand to a rope, at two
o'clock in the morning, 'his right arm dangling by his side.
whilst with his left he jumped up the ship's side, and displayed

a spirit which astonished everyone'. 'Tell the surgeon to get his
instruments ready,' he snapped at them, 'for I know that I must
lose my arm, and the sooner it is off the better.'

Two surgeons carried out the operation, one of them a
Royalist refugee from Toulon. Having administered the usual
tot of rum and put a leathern pad in his mouth to bite on, the
arm was amputated without anaesthetic high up near the
shoulder. A heavy dose of opium was then given. The operation
was done, as was customary, at great speed because of the loss
of blood. The tourniquet used is still preserved at the Wellcome
Medical Historical Museum. Unfortunately, a nerve was taken
up with the ligatures, which it was the custom to leave long for
the purpose of draining the wound.

This mismanagement was to cause him great pain for
several months, and to it was added the nagging fear that there
was no future for a left-handed admiral. He was brought back
to England in the *Seahorse*, where Betsey and Tom Allen, his
faithful 'wally-de-sham', nursed him devotedly. The surgeons
at Bath did him no good, nor did those in London, until he called
in a newly-qualified young man called Michael Jefferson, who
separated the ligatures and the stump healed rapidly. For many
years, however, he suffered phantom pains in the arm.

On 8 December Nelson sent an anonymous note to the
vicar of St George's, Hanover Square : 'An Officer desires to return thanks to Almighty God for his perfect recovery from a
severe wound, and also for many mercies bestowed upon him.'

5 The Nile

On 29 March 1798 Nelson hoisted his flag as Rear-Admiral of the Blue on board H M S *Vanguard*, a two-decker of 74 guns, with Berry as his captain. After spending a few weeks with the fleet at Lisbon, St Vincent ordered him up the Mediterranean on 2 May, thus anticipating instructions from the First Lord which did not reach him till 10 May.

This re-entry of the British into the Mediterranean after an interval of eighteen months marks a turning point in the war. It was caused by intelligence reports that a large armament was fitting out at Toulon and elsewhere. 'The state of affairs', wrote Spencer to St Vincent,

renders it absolutely necessary that the fleet and armament fitting out at Toulon should be prevented from accomplishing its object. ... If you determine to send a detachment, I think it almost unnecessary to suggest to you the propriety of putting it under the command of Sir H. Nelson, whose acquaintance with that part of the world, as well as his activity and disposition, seem to qualify him in a peculiar manner for that service.

To meet what Spencer called 'the great urgency and importance of the measure which has now been determined on', St Vincent placed three 74-gun ships and two frigates under Nelson's command as a squadron of observation, promising him that as soon as reinforcements arrived from England he would send them on, because, in Spencer's words, 'the appearance of a British squadron in the Mediterranean is a condition on which the fate of Europe may at this moment be stated to depend'. Neither the First Lord nor the Prime Minister, however, seemed to have any inkling as to the object of the French. Throughout the winter, after Bonaparte had brought the First Italian Campaign to a brilliant conclusion with the Treaty of Campo Formio in October, rumours of an invasion of Britain had been prevalent. On his return from Italy, the victorious young general had, indeed, been appointed to the Army of England. Proclamations were published that the aim of the Directory was 'to punish the perfidy of the Cabinet of England, that has corrupted the courts of Europe. It is in London that the misfortunes of Europe were planned: it is in London that we must end them.'

Bonaparte, however, took one look at the Channel and decided that such an objective was out of the question. While still in Italy he had proposed to Talleyrand, in charge of Foreign Affairs, that the seizure of Malta would be easy if a fifth column was infiltrated among the Knights of St John. Between them, the prospect of Malta as a stepping stone to Egypt, which might become a French colony to compensate for those lost in the West Indies and also a base for assistance to Tippoo Sahib, Sultan of Mysore, the sworn foe of British rule in India, soon developed. Such an adventure suited the members of the Directory, for nothing could be more embarrassing to them than to have a general of Bonaparte's capacity unemployed in Paris. Approval of the plans was granted on 12 April, with the casual addition that permission was given to build a Suez Canal is necessary.

Bonaparte had his own reasons for looking east rather than north. Convinced by his success in Italy that his star was invincible, his ambition was fanned by stories of Alexander the Great, that other young conqueror. 'Europe is a molehill', the twenty-nine year old general told his secretary. 'Everything wears out: my glory is already past; this tiny Europe does not offer enough of it. We must go to the Orient; all great glory has always been acquired there.' 'In Egypt', he said at the end of his life, 'I felt that I could abandon myself to the most brilliant dreams.'

Such fantasies were beyond the comprehension of the British government. In the summer of 1798, when Bonaparte was well on his way to realizing them, Pitt, Spencer and Dundas were still talking of Naples or Portugal as possible destinations. Pitt thought Ireland the most likely, since that country was in a state of rebellion and a small French force did in fact reach Killala Bay from Brest. In June Dundas admitted, 'just as a fancy of my own', that the French might have designs on India. The fact that Egypt was indeed Bonaparte's objective was not known in London until it was revealed by French newspapers received there on 12 July. Then, when it was also reported that Nelson had failed to find the enemy, panic reigned.

He was dogged by bad luck at the start. On 19 May, soon after arriving off Toulon, a gale blew up which dismasted the *Vanguard* and nearly wrecked her on a shore where the surf could be heard breaking. This forced him to take refuge in southern Sardinia. His frigates, imagining that he must return to Gibraltar for repairs, thereupon deserted him for the rest of the campaign. Lacking the eyes of the fleet, he was helpless. Even without this accident, his three ships would have been useless against a French fleet. Not until Troubridge reinforced him on 7 June, after he had repaired his flagship and returned off Toulon on 31 May, did Nelson have a force of 15 ships of the line and a brig with which he could go in search of the French, whom he now knew were at sea.

My dearest Fanny [he wrote while still off Sardinia]
I ought not to call what has happened to the *Vanguard* by the cold name of accident: I believe firmly that it was the Almighty's goodness to check my consummate vanity. I hope it has made me a better Officer, as I feel confident it had made me a better Man. I kiss the rod with all humility. Figure to yourself a vain man, on Sunday evening at sunset, walking in his cabin with a Squadron about him, who looked up to their Chief to lead them to Glory, and in whom this Chief placed the firmest reliance. . . . Figure to yourself this proud, conceited man when the sun rose on Monday morning, his ship dismasted, his fleet dispersed and himself in such distress that the meanest frigate in France would have been a very unwelcome guest.

During the brief interval of Nelson's absence, Bonaparte's expedition sailed from Toulon on 20 May. Further reinforce-

1   Nelson in 1781 – oil painting by J. F. Rigaud

II and III   Nelson by Collingwood, and Collingwood by
Nelson – two silhouettes of 1785

ments of troops were embarked from Italian ports, so that by the time the *Vanguard* was back on station the French were approaching Sicily. It was an enormous armament, so large that any encounter at sea would have been disastrous, but the secret of its destination had been so well kept, even from the seasick troops on board, that Bonaparte could gamble on a few weeks' grace.

The French fleet of 13 ships of the line and 7 frigates was divided into three divisions under Admiral Brueys in *L'Orient*, a 120-gun three-decker larger than any ship in the Royal Navy and much larger than any of Nelson's two-deckers; Blanquet in the *Franklin*; Villeneuve in the *Guillaume Tell*; and Decrès in a frigate in charge of the convoy of 300 transports with 30,000 infantry on board, 2,800 cavalry, two companies of engineers and 100 field or siege guns. In command were thirty-one generals, six of whom became Napoleon's marshals and one (Murat) a king – such men as Junot, Berthier, Desaix, Kléber, Menou (who turned Muslim), Dumas the huge mulatto cavalry leader who became the father of the novelist. Since Egypt was to be colonized, and since Bonaparte had been immensely flattered by his recent election to the Institute (as the Academy was called after the Revolution), 167 *savants* were included – mathematicians, engineers, mineralogists, chemists, artists – under the enthusiastic leadership of Gaspard Monge, already an expert in plunder as the acquisition of the Mona Lisa for the Louvre testifies. It is hard to say whether the organization and embarkation of this force in ten weeks, or the secrecy about its destination, is the more remarkable.

On 9 June the French were at Malta, which, in spite of its formidable fortifications and traditions of heroic sieges, surrendered without a blow two days later. The fifth column among the French Knights had done its work well. During the next week, while Monge stowed the loot on board the flagship, Bonaparte reorganized the island with a stream of orders and proclamations. On 18 June the fleet put to sea again, *L'Orient* loaded with three tons of plate, the Cathedral gates and twelve statues of the Apostles made of silver. General Vaubois was left to hold the island, which he did with extraordinary courage for the next two years against both the Maltese and their new British allies. The stay at Malta was brief because Bonaparte knew that an English squadron was at his heels, though under whose command and of what size he was ignorant.

Only after they had put to sea were the troops informed that their destination was Egypt:

Soldiers! You are about to undertake a conquest whose effects on the world's civilization and trade are incalculable. You will inflict upon England a blow which is certain to wound her in her most sensitive spot, while waiting for the day when you can deal her a death blow. We shall make some wearisome marches; we shall fight a few battles; we shall succeed in all our enterprises; destiny is for us. The Mameluke beys, who exclusively favour English trade, who have oppressed our merchants with vexations, and who are tyrannizing over the unhappy people of the Nile valley, will cease to exist a few days after our landing. The people with whom we shall live are Mohammedans. Their chief creed is this: 'There is no God but God, and Mohammed is His prophet.' Do not contradict them . . .

Where Napoleon led, Nelson had to follow. Once he had been reinforced, he was off in chase, though without the essential frigates. News that Malta had fallen was gained from Sir William Hamilton at the Court of Naples. From that moment the conviction that Egypt was Bonaparte's destination, and that he had designs on India, gained on him. He was thus the first to have any intuition of Bonaparte's plans. On 17 June, when he heard about Malta, he assured St Vincent that 'I will bring the French fleet to action the moment I can lay my hands on them.' To Spencer he wrote: 'I shall believe they are going on their scheme for possessing Alexandria, and getting troops to India. . . . Be they bound for the Antipodes, your Lordship may rely that I will not lose a moment in bringing them to action.'

With the support of his captains, whose advice he sought, he sailed for Alexandria. Then occurred the second accident which made this the most frustrating chase in his career. The French and British fleets passed each other during the night of 22–23 June, the latter overtaking the former by its superior rate of sailing, but, because there were no scouting frigates, never guessing that the huge French fleet was within a few kilometres of them. Some French officers even declared that they heard the sound of signal guns. The consequence was that he sighted the Pharos of Alexandria on 29 June to find no sign of the French there.

In a self-justificatory letter to St Vincent which he wrote that day he explains why he had stretched so far east without orders. He says that both he and his officers were convinced that Egypt was the goal of the enemy, but as there was no sign of them he must stand or fall by that guess: 'I am before your Lordship's judgement (which in the present case I feel is the Tribunal of my Country) and if, under all circumstances, it is decided that I am wrong, I ought, for the sake of my Country, to be superseded.'

Without more delay he carried on to the coasts of the Levant, skirting the south coast of Crete. Twenty-four hours later, on 1 July, the French appeared at Alexandria and within a few hours were masters of the town. During the remainder of that month, while Bonaparte was leading his army south on its terrible march across the desert to defeat the Mamelukes at the battle of the Pyramids on 29 July, thus securing the possession of Cairo, Nelson was circling the eastern Mediterranean in a vain search for the French fleet.

Back at Syracuse on 20 July he admitted himself baffled: 'I cannot find, or this moment learn, beyond vague conjecture, where the French fleet are gone to', he told Hamilton. 'All my ill fortune, hitherto, has proceeded from want of frigates'. Another letter to St Vincent of the same date shows how keenly he felt the disappointment:

Every moment I have to regret the frigates having left me, to which may be attributed my ignorance of the movements of the enemy. Your Lordship deprived yourself of frigates to make mine certainly the finest squadron in the world, and I feel that I have the zeal and activity to do credit to your appointment, and yet to be unsuccessful hurts me most sensibly. But if they are above water, I will find them out, and if possible bring them to Battle.

A few days later Troubridge arrived with a French wine brig in tow bringing news that a month earlier the French had been seen off Crete, steering south-east. So Nelson had been right after all. It is difficult in these days to appreciate how wide the seas were before the invention of steam or radio. The search might go on for weeks, however large the force, before it could be located by slow sailing ships taking days to cover a distance which a steamship, not to mention an aircraft, could cover in a few hours.

Hence it was not until the morning of 1 August that Nelson was back at Alexandria again. There he learned that Brueys had anchored his fleet in Aboukir Bay eight kilometres (five miles) to the eastward. Without a moment's pause he continued under sail with his ships in no sort of order so that the fastest might find them first. At 2 p.m. they were seen by the French rounding the point of Aboukir Island, on which a fort had been established. At six o'clock the battle commenced.

The Battle of the Nile, as it came to be called, appears to be the most spontaneous in naval warfare. But it must not be forgotten that during the long days spent in the chase it was Nelson's habit to invite his captains on board the *Vanguard* to discuss tactics with them. In the account of the battle which Berry wrote under the pseudonym of 'An Officer of Rank' he says that the Admiral, having the highest opinion of his captains, used to discuss in detail 'his own ideas of the different and best modes of attack, and such plans as he prepared to execute upon falling in with the enemy, whatever their position or situation might be, by day or night'. Among the Band of Brothers, only Collingwood was absent because he was on duty with the fleet off Cadiz. All those who were now with Nelson were old friends and comrades in arms. They pooled their ideas while Nelson explained his own, especially an attack by concentrating on the most vulnerable part of the enemy line. A loose order of sailing enabled the fastest sailers to lead and since every captain could be depended on to seize any opportunity that offered, signals could be dispensed with once battle was joined. Nelson was confident that any British ship could engage any Frenchman with advantage, and that since numbers were roughly equal (excluding the French frigates, which in any case never lay in the line), and since impetuosity and surprise were dominating factors, victory was certain.

It was different with the French. In the only letter which Bonaparte received from Brueys, the latter complained that all his best men had been taken for the Army, and since his ships were so short of water and provisions landing parties had to be sent daily to obtain supplies from this desert coast inhabited by hostile Bedouin. All that he could do, since the Old Port of Alexandria was not navigable, and since he had not been given permission to leave the coast, was to anchor his fleet in as strong a position as possible to await the inevitable British attack. Bonaparte (as was his habit) was quick to blame his admiral for the disaster that followed, and at St Helena he had the effrontery to pretend that Nelson owed his victory to the negligence of the captains in the van and 'the poor conduct of Admiral Villeneuve' in the rear, who could have turned the affair into a French victory the next day had he not run away. But it was Bonaparte himself who compelled Brueys to stay on the coast.

The French position was not as strong as was imagined. Brueys had anchored his ships in a 1½-kilometre long line shaped like a bow, with his flagship marking the centre. Anticipating an attack on his rear from the open side of the bay, he placed his frigates inside to strengthen it. To protect the van he mounted batteries along the shore, but their range proved too short. He relied for his real defence on the shoals inside the point. The mistake was made to moor the ships too far apart in order to give them room to swing, so that the leading ship, *Guerrier*, was some 200 metres from her anchor buoy. 'The position of the enemy presented the most formidable obstacles,' wrote Berry, 'but the Admiral viewed these with the eye of a seaman determined on attack; and it instantly struck his eager and penetrating mind that where there was room for an enemy's ship to swing, there was room for one of our's to anchor.'

Nevertheless the credit for the opening move must go to Captain Foley, whose *Goliath* was sailing in company with

The Battle of the Nile

TO ALEXANDRIA

ABOUKIR

FORT

SHOALS

French ships   British ships

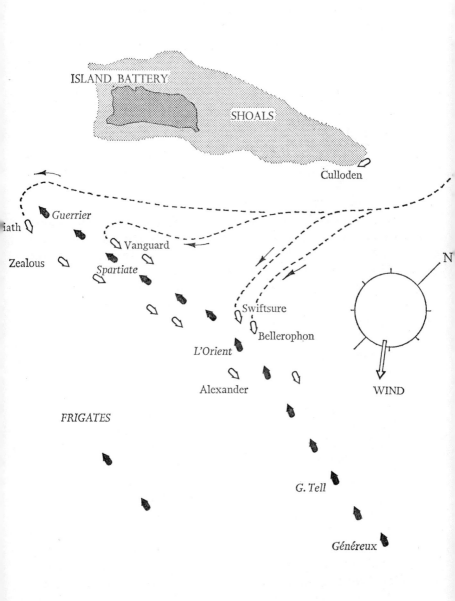

1 *August* 1798

ISLAND BATTERY

SHOALS

Culloden

iath

Guerrier

Zealous

Vanguard

Spartiate

N

Swiftsure

Bellerophon

L'Orient

WIND

Alexander

FRIGATES

G. Tell

Généreux

BATTERY

Samuel Hood's *Zealous* some way ahead of the main body as they rounded the island. George Elliot, the signal midshipman perched on the royal yard of the former, was the first to see the enemy fleet. Fearing that if he hailed the deck the *Zealous* would overhear him and contest the honour of leading the fleet into action, he slid down the backstay to report. By the time he reached the deck, the *Zealous* had also sighted the enemy and signalled to the ships astern of her. The two ships raced in to attack the van, the *Goliath* leading by a length.

Foley had the inestimable advantage of having on board a chart – Bellini's *Petit Atlas Maritime* – which, though forty years old, was much more accurate than the English one which Hood possessed. In those days, before charts were issued to ships, captains had to find their own charts. Elliot says that he heard Foley tell the Master, who was responsible for navigating the ship, that he wished to get inside the French line, partly because he guessed that side of the French ships would not be manned: 'I immediately looked for the buoy on her anchor and saw it apparently at the usual distance of a cable's length, which I reported; they both looked at it and agreed that there was room to pass between the ship and her anchor; the danger was the ship being close up to the edge of the shoal, but it was decided to do it.'

Brueys never thought that Nelson would dare to attack so late in the evening: it was too late to start a battle without the confusion of a night action and the English were in no sort of a line as they rounded the cape in a bunch. Troubridge in the *Culloden* was some way astern towing a prize and in trying to catch up cut the corner too sharply so that she ran ashore and missed the action altogether. Yet here were two ships leading inside the French line, followed by the *Audacious*, *Theseus* and *Orion*, according to Nelson's preconceived notion of doubling the line and, 'by attacking the van and centre, the wind blowing directly along their line, I was enabled to throw what force I pleased on a few ships'.

As we entered the bay we stripped to our trousers, opened our ports, cleared, and every ship we passed gave them a broadside and three cheers . . . [wrote John Nicol, a seaman, adding an interesting touch that, as his action station was at the powder magazine] I was much indebted to the gunner's wife, who gave her husband and me a drink of wine every now and then, which lessened our fatigue

The first ship to attack on the seaward side was the *Vanguard*, the sixth in order of attack, which engaged the *Spartiate*, lying third in the enemy line. This was done to enable the ships following her to reach towards the centre in the fading light. As his officers rose from the table to go to their stations, Nelson exclaimed 'Before this time tomorrow, I shall have gained a Peerage or Westminster Abbey!' It was nearly the latter. Soon after engaging the *Spartiate*, which defended herself stoutly, he was hit on the forehead by a langridge shot which caused an eight-centimetre cut, laying bare his skull. A flap of skin fell over his eye, totally blinding him with the flow of blood. He was led below, where he took his turn in the surgeon's cockpit. Much later he was taken up on deck to witness the destruction of the French flagship, but felt faint and had to be taken below again. Ever afterwards he wore a lock of his hair long to hide the scar.

Though many of their men were still on shore on watering parties, the French defended themselves vigorously. The *Vanguard* was hard pressed by the *Spartiate* and *Aquilon* until Captain Louis in the *Minotaur* sailed past to engage the latter. But it was the three-decked *L'Orient* which caused the most damage. The *Bellerophon* which first attacked her, was driven off badly damaged after an hour's fighting. Two reserve ships, *Swiftsure* and *Alexander* then came to on either side of her, the latter cutting through the French line. Brueys and his captain, Casabianca, fought the ship magnificently, even after the former had lost both his legs and was then literally cut in two by a shot as he directed operations from a chair on the quarterdeck. Unfortunately for him, several oil jars which had been in use for painting ship had been left lying about. A blaze sprang up and the *Swiftsure* pumped her fire into it. About ten o'clock, soon after Brueys was killed, the fire spread and the huge ship exploded. The sound was heard and the flames seen in the darkness as far away as Alexandria on the one side and Rosetta on the other.

All accounts agree that after this awe-inspiring incident there was a lull in the fighting lasting for some time until Vice-Admiral Blanquet's *Franklin* resumed firing. But the loss of the *L'Orient* virtually meant the end of the battle. By next morning only three ships in the rear – Villeneuve's *Guillaume Tell*, *Généreux* and *Timoléon* – were left. They got under sail to escape, but the last-named ran aground, so that of Brueys's original 13 ships only 2 survived. As for the battlefield, it is sufficient to quote John Nicol once more: 'Went on deck to view the state of the fleets, and an awful sight it was. The whole bay was covered with dead bodies, mangled, wounded and scorched, not a bit of clothes on them except their trousers.'

Casualty figures are never very accurate, but Nelson reckoned that 9,000 men were taken or killed in the 11 enemy ships. In his own fleet 218 men were killed and 677 wounded, including himself. Such was the victory which he announced in a noble despatch to St Vincent:

My Lord, Almighty God has blessed his Majesty's arms in the late Battle, by a great victory over the Fleet of the Enemy, who I attacked at sunset on 1 August off the Mouth of the Nile. The Enemy was moored in a strong line of Battle for defending the entrance of the Bay of Shoals, flanked by numerous Gunboats, four Frigates and a Battery of Guns and Mortars on an Island in their Van; but nothing could withstand the Squadron your Lordship did me the honour to place under my command. Their high state of Discipline is well known to you, and with the judgement of the Captains, together with their Valour, and that of the Officers and Men of every description, it was absolutely irresistible. Could anything from my pen add to the character of the Captains, I would write it with pleasure, but that is impossible.

The day after the battle Nelson recommended his captains to hold thanksgiving services on board their ships. When Bonaparte heard the news of the defeat he faced his officers to electrify them (according to his own account) with these words: 'Well, gentlemen, now we are obliged to accomplish great things: we shall accomplish them. We must found a great empire, and we shall found it. The sea, of which we are no longer masters, separates us from our homeland, but no sea separates us from either Africa or Asia.'

Nelson's comment on the immediate result of his victory was more realistic: 'Their Army is in a scrape, and will not get out of it.' His biographer is not directly concerned with Bonaparte's attempts to do so – the extraordinary march to Jaffa and Acre, where resistance inspired by Sir Sidney Smith and the outbreak of plague forced him to retreat to Cairo again; the way he deserted his army to escape back to France and carry out the *coup d'état* of 18th Brumaire against the Directory; the final surrender of the Army of Egypt after the amphibious landing made in Aboukir Bay (where the masts of *L'Orient* could still be seen in the water three years later) by Admiral Lord Keith and General Sir Ralph Abercromby in 1801.

For the broader political consequences of so complete a victory we need go no further than a letter from Poussielgue, who was what we should now call Paymaster of the Forces in Egypt and had recently been one of those who undermined the resistance of Malta:

The fatal engagement ruined all our hopes; it prevented us from receiving the remainder of the forces which were destined for us; it left the field free for the English to persuade the Port to declare war against us; it rekindled that which was barely extinguished in the heart of the Austrian Emperor; it opened the Mediterranean to the Russians, and planted them on our frontiers; it occasioned the loss of Italy and the invaluable possessions in the Adriatic which we owed to the successful campaign of Bonaparte, and finally it rendered abortive all our projects, since it was no longer possible for us to dream of giving the English any uneasiness in India. Added to this was the effect on the people of Egypt, whom we wished to consider as friends and allies. They became our enemies, and, entirely surrounded as we were by Turks, we found ourselves engaged in a most difficult defensive war, without a glimpse of the slightest advantage to be obtained from it.

As far as Nelson himself was concerned, the fruits of victory were overwhelming. When we recall the fact that his head wound was more serious than was at first imagined and that the adulations which now rained down on him from every court in Europe would have affected a much more modest man than he was, the psychological crisis he was to undergo during the next few months may be better understood. It is the saddest part of his life to describe, because it brought out the worst in him, but undoubtedly he himself saw it as the happiest and the most triumphant.

The honours and rewards showered upon him are of intriguing interest. His captains gave him a jewelled sword, with the request to have his portrait painted. Ben Hallowell made him the macabre present of a coffin fashioned from the mainmast of *L'Orient*, 'that when you are tired of this life you may be buried in one of your own trophies'. Nelson kept it in his cabin for a long time and in the event he was indeed buried in it. The treasure of the Knights of St John, which had been stowed on board the same ship, went down with her to await the researches of some future underwater archaeologist. As for the Sultan, he gave Nelson a Chelengk, or Plume of Triumph, a diamond spray which he wore in his hat, as Abbott's well-known portrait shows. A few years ago, however, this relic was stolen from a museum and has never been recovered.

His first duty after the battle was to send despatches to all interested parties. The first despatch was to be brought home by H M S *Leander*, but she was captured off Crete by the *Généreux*, one of the two ships which escaped the holocaust at the Nile. On board the *Mutine* brig Lieutenant Capel took another copy to Naples and thence to London. Another was sent to India via the Persian Gulf. Saumarez, escorting the prizes, was ordered to inform Malta and demand the surrender of the island, where he was rudely rebuffed by General Vaubois. Having left Hood in command of a small blockading squadron, Nelson himself took the *Vanguard* and other ships to Naples.

When the news of victory reached London on 2 October, the town went mad with joy. As the Duchess of Devonshire said, 'He has turned all our heads.' The illuminations on an unprecedented scale are reflected in Lady Spencer's letter to the new national hero who, as he once hoped, at last had a gazette to himself:

Captain Capel just arrived! Joy, joy, joy to you, brave, gallant, immortalised Nelson! May that great God, whose cause you so valiantly support, protect and bless you to the end of your career! Such a race surely never was run. My heart is absolutely bursting with different sensations of joy, of gratitude, of pride, of every emotion that ever warmed the bosom of a British woman, on hearing of her Country's glory – and all produced by you, my dear, my good friend. This moment that guns are firing, illuminations are preparing, your gallant name is echoed from street to street, and every Briton feels his obligations to you weighing him down.

If her language seems somewhat inflated to the modern reader, it is worth recalling that her husband, First Lord of the Admiralty and one of the leading peers of the realm, fell flat on the floor at the news. Down at Burnham Thorpe the event was celebrated by roasting a sheep, while at Bath Nelson's father could only say that 'he soars in spheres unknown to private stations': his son was now Baron Nelson of the Nile and of Burnham Thorpe in the County of Norfolk.

The congratulations which most flattered his professional pride came from Lord Howe, the victor of the Glorious First of June and now Admiral of the Fleet. Howe having offered his compliments on 'this singular occasion, not less remarkable for the skill than the cool judgement testified under considerable disadvantages in the superior force and situation of the enemy which you had to surmount,' Nelson replied with one of his best letters: 'I had the happiness to command a Band of Brothers; therefore night was to my advantage. Each knew his duty, and I was sure each would feel for a French ship.' After outlining the tactics employed and acknowledging his debt to the man who had introduced the new system of signalling into the Navy, he concludes by saying that he had not hitherto detailed the action to anyone, 'but I should have thought it wrong to have kept it from one who is our great master in naval tactics and bravery'.

The most hysterical of the victory celebrations awaited him at Naples, which he reached on 22 September. It is typical of his worldly innocence as well as of his vanity that the most vivid description of what took place occurs in two letters to his wife:

My dearest Fanny,

It is hardly possible to know where to begin. My head is almost turned by letters already and what am I to expect when I get on shore? My head is healed and I am better. The Kingdom of the Two Sicilies are mad with joy: from the throne to the peasant all are alike. From Lady Hamilton's letter the situation of the Queen was truly pitiable. I only hope I shall not have to be a witness to a renewal of it. I give you Lady Hamilton's words: 'How shall I describe the transports of the Queen? 'Tis not possible. She fainted, cried, kissed her husband, her children, walked frantic about the room, cried, kissed and embraced any persons near exclaiming "Oh brave Nelson. Oh God bless and protect our brave deliverer! Oh Nelson, Nelson, what do we not owe you! Oh Victor, Saviour of Italy . . .

Emma was not to be outdone herself. She and Sir William rowed out with a hundred other boats when the *Vanguard* came to an anchor in the bay. As she came up the side to be introduced to the hero:

Up flew her Ladyship and exclaiming 'Oh God, is it possible!' fell into my arm more dead than alive. Tears, however, soon set matters to rights, when alongside came the King. The scene was in its way affecting. He took me by the hand, calling me his deliverer and preserver, with every other expression of kindness. In short, all Naples calls me *nostra liberatore*, for the scene with the lower classes was truly affecting. I hope one day to have the pleasure of introducing you to Lady Hamilton. She is one of the very best women in this world.

6 Emma

The story of Emy Lyon, who later called herself Emily Hart and became Emma, Lady Hamilton, is almost as well known today as that of Lord Nelson, partly because of its extraordinary nature, partly on account of the insatiable popular interest in one of the world's greatest romances. Though chat about Emma is largely irrelevant to an account of Nelson as a public character, because he loved her so deeply and because her influence certainly affected his career, no modern biographer can ignore it as earlier writers could do before the true facts were known.

The strikingly beautiful girl who became the wife of the British plenipotentiary at the court of Naples was seduced (probably by a naval officer) at the age of sixteen, when she was a servant. She became a model advertising a dubious Temple of Health, where she began to develop those poses which she called her 'attitudes', famous throughout Europe by constant repetition. The Hon. Charles Greville made her his mistress at a time when Romney was painting her in his most seductive and sentimental manner. When Greville in 1786 found himself compelled 'to reduce my establishment', he passed her on to his aging uncle Sir William Hamilton, then ambassador to the court of the Two Sicilies.

Emma genuinely loved Greville. Appalled at his desertion when she was only twenty-one and Sir William was fifty-six, she wrote in one of her sprawling ungrammatical letters:

I have lived with you five years and you have sent me to a strange place and no one prospect, me thinking you was coming to me; instead of which I was told to live, you know how, with Sir W. No, I respect him, but no, never, shall he perhaps live with me for a

little while like you and send me to England, then what am I to do,
what is to become of me?

Sir William, who was respected as a diplomat and widely
known as a connoisseur of Greek vases (among them the Port-
land Vase which so strongly influenced the Wedgwood style),
treated her at first as just another *objet d'art*. As his friend Beck-
ford told him, 'I look upon you as the first of connoisseurs –
not only in the fine arts, but in the science of human felicity.'
But Emma was determined on marriage, a course which her
mother (now known as Mrs Cadogan) supported with all the
instincts of a bawd. In five years she was clever enough to succeed because she adapted herself so easily to the style of an
ambassadress, giving life to a decadent court by her good looks
and astounding vitality, at the same time developing a soprano
voice which was admired even in Naples. Goethe called her 'a
masterpiece of the arch-artist', adding that 'in her, Hamilton
finds the charm of all antiques, the fair profiles on Sicilian coins,
the Apollo Belvidere himself . . .'. When Casanova heard that Sir
William, in Horace Walpole's words, had 'married his gallery
of statues', he solemnly remarked that such a fate often over-
takes a man of intelligence when he grows old. 'It is always a
mistake to marry, but when a man's physical and mental forces
are declining, it is a calamity.'

He was wrong. Sir William, with the healthy cynicism of
his century, fully realized that one day he would be 'superannuated', but in the meantime she made him happy and comfortable. 'You would be delighted to see how happy we are,' she
wrote, 'no quarrelling, nor crossness, nor caprice, all nonsense
is at an end and every body that sees us are edified by our example of conjugal and domestic felicaty.'

Such was the ménage into which the Hero of the Nile in-
truded when he landed at Naples. When Sir William heard of his
wound, he had told him that 'a pleasant apartment is ready for
you at my house, and Emma is looking out for the softest pillows
to repose the few wearied limbs you have left'. It cannot have
been long before the nurse became the mistress, the oddest
feature of the whole affair being that Sir William, who must

iv   Lady Hamilton in 1800 – pastel by J. H. Schmidt

On the back Emma wrote: 'This portrait of Emma
Hamilton was in all the actions with the virtuous gallant
and heroic Nelson. He called it his Guardian Angel and
thought he could not be victorious if he did not see it in
the midst of battle.'

v   Nelson in 1801 – oil sketch by Sir William Beechey

have been aware of what was happening, accepted the situation without ever allowing his self-respect to lessen his admiration for his guest. The three became, as Emma loved to put it, adapting the motto of the Order of the Bath, *tria juncta in uno*. Each of them continued to display the attributes of the class from which each sprang. Sir William continued to be the detached aristocrat of exquisite taste and irony, Nelson the passionate professional officer in whom ambition vied with patriotism, and Emma the gay, vulgar, gushing hostess. But they were all getting older, Sir William more infirm, Nelson more vain and Emma's beauty fading into a blowsy middle age.

Before he became entrammelled in its intrigues, Nelson described Naples as 'a country of fiddlers and poets, whores and scoundrels'. Unlike Burnham Thorpe, it was the ideal setting for an illicit love affair. Presiding over the court were King Ferdinand, a Bourbon beloved of the *lazzaroni* and despised for his boorishness by the aristocracy since his only interests were hunting, drinking and wenching, and the Habsburg Queen Maria Carolina, who shared all the political stupidity of her sister Marie Antoinette and none of her charm. Her forceful character led Napoleon to describe her as the only man in Naples. The fate which overtook the royal family in France served to strengthen her reactionary prejudices, so that she and Nelson were united in their detestation of the Jacobins. Emma, dominating both of them by her overwhelming personality, fanned their prejudices with flattery. It was just the sort of régime which was being overthrown all over Europe, so that it was only a matter of time before the French reached Naples. The pity was that for the next two years Nelson's growing passion for Emma made him insist that this rotten state must be protected at all costs.

For the whole of that time he was a sick man, constantly complaining that his head was splitting with pain, or laid low by recurrent bouts of malaria. He was evidently suffering from delayed effects of concussion, but he was so infatuated that he could not resist the round of nocturnal parties, dances and gambling sessions in which Emma delighted, while at the same time trying to concern himself with the multifarious problems of the eastern and central Mediterranean, in which he was now senior officer. In such circumstances it is not surprising that his letters to his wife became fewer and briefer, and that for the only time in his life he was reprimanded for neglecting his duty.

Not that he was by any means idle during those months: his extensive correspondence proves the contrary. In those days, when communications were so slow, an admiral had also to be something of a diplomat. Nelson's victory multiplied the objectives of British policy in the Mediterranean. It was necessary, in the first place, to continue the watch on Alexandria and to impede the progress of the French army along the coast road to Acre, when Bonaparte tried to escape by way of Syria. As new allies appeared upon the scene, it was essential to cooperate with them – the Turkish fleet, a Russian squadron under Admiral Oushakoff ('a blackguard' in Nelson's view) which seized Corfu and had an eye on Malta, the Austrian army which now reappeared in northern Italy. As Malta stubbornly held out under Vaubois, Captain Ball was put in command of the blockading squadron until the island surrendered and he became its first governor. Minorca was occupied in order to provide, at Port Mahon, an essential base in the western Mediterranean, in case the Spanish fleet escaped from Cadiz or the Brest fleet entered that sea in order to help the army stranded in Egypt. To cope with these manifold tasks St Vincent remained with the main fleet at Gibraltar, Nelson being responsible for the protection of Naples and Sicily as well as the guardian of Italy in general and the supervisor of the blockade of Malta, while two ships were sent under the command of Sir Sidney Smith to the Levant.

It was this action, together with Smith's assumption of the title of Commodore, which annoyed Nelson most. He regarded it as an infringement on his command and he shared with other naval officers a dislike of the flamboyant style of the self-appointed Commodore. Two such theatrical characters could not avoid a clash: if Nelson loved to wear all his medals all the time, Sir Sidney must be the only man to have galloped down Whitehall in full Turkish dress to announce his own success. But Nelson need not have worried. The First Lord pointed out that it was all a misunderstanding: Smith had not been given the authority of a real commodore, so that he remained under Nelson's orders. Having taken the opportunity of reprimanding him severely for issuing passports to French civilians who wished to return from Alexandria, Nelson was the first to congratulate Smith on his brilliant defence of Acre, which compelled Bonaparte to retreat to Cairo.

It was in the affairs of Naples that Nelson displayed such a notable lack of political sense, as well as of personal dignity. With Emma always at his side, no wonder his zeal for the public service somewhat relaxed.

His first mistake was to persuade the King to occupy Rome, now that the Austrian army in the north had temporarily thrown the French on the defensive. Ferdinand did so, but within a few weeks he was back again at Naples with the French at his heels. Since it was only a matter of time before they entered the capital, Nelson persuaded the royal family that a secret escape to Palermo on board the flagship was the only course to take.

Two days before Christmas they came on board the *Foudroyant* with vast quantities of baggage and treasure labelled 'Stores for Nelson' reputed to be worth £2½ million. Sir William sent his precious collection home in H M S *Colossus*, which was wrecked off the Scillies, though much of the collection was saved and is now in the British Museum.

It was a fearful voyage to Palermo in terrible weather. A six-year-old prince died in Lady Hamilton's arms. Once in Sicily, however, Ferdinand took himself off hunting, while the Queen and Emma organized the usual round of parties, a notable one being to celebrate the marriage of the aged Prime Minister to his fourteen-year-old niece. A succession of such festivities did nothing to restore Nelson's health.

In April 1799, with the French at Naples and no one knowing whether they would march further south, the news that Admiral Bruix had escaped with the Brest fleet and was on his way to the Mediterranean came like a clap of thunder. Admiral Lord Keith prevented him from joining up with the Spaniards at

Cadiz, but they passed the Straits under the eyes of the commander-in-chief to reach Toulon. St Vincent was a sick man who
had to turn over the command to Keith in the middle of the
crisis, so that the latter followed them to Nice, whence Bruix
intended to proceed along the coast to Genoa. However, when
he heard that the English fleet was after him, he turned west to
return to Brest, though he now had 43 ships to Keith's 31.

Not realizing that the French admiral was throwing away
the one chance of a success at sea during the Revolutionary war
– that of superiority in numbers as well as in intiative – Keith
imagined that Minorca was in danger, and possibly Gibraltar.
He ordered Nelson to go at once to the defence of the island.
Nelson refused to move, on the grounds that he believed

the safety of the Kingdom of Naples depends at the present moment
on my detaining my squadron, as I have no scruple in deciding that
it is better to save the Kingdom of Naples and risk Minorca, than to
risk the Kingdom of Naples to save Minorca. Your Lordship will, I
hope, approve of my decision.

Keith did not approve. Nor did St Vincent. Nor did the
Admiralty. For the only occasion in his life, Nelson was officially
reprimanded. He was told that their Lordships could not see
'sufficient reason to justify you having disobeyed the orders
you have received from your commanding officer, or having
left Minorca exposed to the risk of being attacked'. The mes-
sage stung him. But the pill was sugared when he was left in
temporary command while Keith followed the enemy north to
Brest in case something was intended against Ireland.

Meanwhile events were taking place in Naples which Nelson's detractors have seized upon as one of the very few occasions on which it is possible to impugn his honour. When he and
the King returned to Naples on board the *Foudroyant* it was
found that Cardinal Ruffo, who had won back the capital with
his own army, had signed what Nelson regarded as 'infamous
terms' with the Jacobins, so much so that the Queen was convinced that the Cardinal was a Jacobin himself. Ruffo had always
been jealous of Nelson's ascendancy at court, especially since

the King had put him in command of the Neapolitan navy. Because neither the King nor Nelson believed in treating with the French, they annulled the armistice as soon as they anchored in the bay. Unconditional surrender was what they demanded, but they found that Ruffo had already signed not an armistice but a capitulation on specific terms. The dissident faction in the city gave themselves up, trusting not only to those terms but to the clemency of their sovereign. Among them was the distinguished admiral Prince Caracciolo, who had learned his profession on board English ships. He had received the King's permission to return to Naples to see to his own affairs, but had there been persuaded to take command of the republican fleet and in that capacity had fired on a royalist vessel.

When the French left, Caracciolo fled in disguise, but he was recognized by peasants and brought on board the *Foudroyant* in handcuffs. Nelson immediately signalled the captain of the Neapolitan frigate *Minerva* to assemble a court martial. Under martial law, Caracciolo was certainly guilty. By noon sentence was passed by a court at which no defence witnesses were called and at five o'clock his body could be seen from the flagship hanging from the frigate's yard arm.

According to Nelson's enemies, he and Lady Hamilton dined well that night and even rowed round the bay to have another look at Caracciolo's body. A few days later it was said that the body of the dead admiral bobbed up in the water just astern of the flagship, his white hair floating on the waves.

One need not accept such stories, even though it must be admitted that Nelson, a man noted for his humanity in war, showed no mercy on this occasion. It is clear that political passion and the malign influence of the Queen and her confidante, Emma, blinded him to the true situation. He imagined that he was saving Naples from a Red Terror. What actually occurred was a White Terror, the blame for which has been unfairly laid on his shoulders. The unseemly haste with which the judicial murder was executed by the Prince's own countrymen is a reminder that these were brutal times. Only two days before, a marine on board Nelson's own ship had been sentenced to death for threatening an officer, and a seaman had received 250 lashes with a cat-o'-nine-tails for looting. Yet it must be recorded that shortly after the disgraceful Caracciolo incident Nelson was created Duke of Brontë in Sicily, supposed to be worth £3,000 a year, though he never received a penny from it.

It is pleasant to pass to an episode in which Nelson appears in his old colours – the capture of the *Généreux* on 18 February 1800. She and the *Guillaume Tell* were the only ships to escape at the Nile, and Blackwood was soon to tell Nelson that the latter had been taken when trying to escape from Malta. The former had captured the *Leander* when she was carrying Nelson's despatches, and with them his favourite flag-captain, Sir Edward Berry. Berry was now back on board Nelson's new flagship, *Foudroyant*.

When the *Généreux* was sighted through the mist that morning, the *Northumberland* was leading the chase. 'This will not do, Sir Ed'ard,' said Nelson to Berry in his high, slightly nasal voice. 'We must and shall beat the *Northumberland*.' The *Foudroyant*'s flag-captain immediately ordered all possible steps to increase the speed of the ship, wetting the sails, slacking the stays to give the masts more play, pumping out the ship. Meanwhile the admiral walked the quarter-deck with rapid steps, 'working his fin', that is to say moving the stump of his arm, a well-known sign of impatience.

'A strange sail ahead of the chase', called the look-out man in the bows. A midshipman was promptly ordered to the masthead with a telescope. 'A sloop of war or a frigate', was his report. When her number was demanded, she turned out to be the frigate *Success*, Captain Peard. Nelson told her to cut off the flying enemy. Though he knew that the odds were heavily against him, Captain Peard fired a broadside against the French line-of-battle ship. Nelson applauded his courage, knowing that a single broadside from the *Généreux* might sink the frigate. When the smoke cleared, it was seen that the *Success* had been crippled, but she continued to pursue the enemy. 'She has done well for her size', said Nelson. 'Try a shot from the lower deck at her, Sir Ed'ard.' The first shot was seen to go over the enemy ship, proving that she was well within range. The order was therefore given for slow, deliberate sighting shots while the men ran to their battle stations ('beat to quarters' was the order to the drummers).

Within a few minutes the *Foudroyant*'s shots began to tell. As soon as the enemy's tricolour was hauled down, Nelson gave the order to cease fire. A boat was lowered and Berry was granted his wish to take his own revenge by boarding the prize himself. He returned with the sword of the French admiral, who had been killed by a shot from the *Success*. 'This makes nineteen sail of the line and four admirals I have been present at the capture of', wrote the delighted Nelson, at the same time paying tribute to Peard's gallantry in throwing his frigate across the path of such a large enemy ship.

Nelson's behaviour on shore at this period of his life naturally aroused comment on the part of his naval brethren. Keith was no doubt expressing his views as a dour Scot when he told his sister that he was 'cutting the most absurd figure possible for folly and vanity'. General Sir John Moore summarized the Queen succinctly as 'a bitch' and went on to describe Nelson as 'covered with stars, ribbons and medals, more like a Prince in an opera than the Conqueror of the Nile'. Even so steadfast a friend as Troubridge warned him that 'your Lordship is a stranger to half that happens and the talk it occasions. If you knew what your friends feel for you, I am sure you would cut out all the nocturnal parties.' Such talk reached London until the point came when Spencer decided that he must be recalled, which he did in a tactful private letter:

It is by no means my intention to call you away from service, but having observed that you have been under the necessity of quitting your station off Malta on account of the state of your health, which I am persuaded you could not have thought of doing without such necessity, it appeared to me much more advisable for you to come home at once, than to be obliged to remain inactive at Palermo.

So, in the spring of 1800, Nelson and the Hamiltons, the Queen, the inevitable Mrs Cadogan, Miss Cornelia Knight (an ageing spinster who was the daughter of an admiral), and the faithful Tom Allen decided to return from Leghorn. Nelson asked Keith if the party might go home in the *Foudroyant*. The commander-in-chief naturally refused to withdraw an 80-gun ship on such a service and offered him a frigate instead. Nelson considered such a small ship unsuitable, so it was decided to go overland via Vienna, Prague, Dresden and Hamburg.

It was a strange triumphal progress. Wherever he went the populace gave him a hero's welcome, while eyebrows were raised among the upper classes at his extraordinary behaviour. At Vienna Josef Haydn, *kapellmeister* to Prince Esterhazy, an old Naples acquaintance, was already his devoted admirer. Having just completed his finest Mass, that in D Minor, he re-named it the Nelson Mass after hearing the news of Aboukir. Now, at Emma's request, he composed an aria with nauseating words by Miss Knight, which Emma sang and then, leaving the old man to conduct the rest of the concert, retired to the next room to play faro with Nelson.

At Dresden a hawk-eyed gossip named Mrs St George left an unflattering description of them :

Dined at Mr Elliot's with only the Nelson party. It is plain that Lord Nelson thinks of nothing but Lady Hamilton, who is totally occupied by the same subject. She is bold, forward, coarse, assuming and vain. Her figure is colossal, but, excepting her feet, which are hideous, well shaped. Her bones are large, and she is exceedingly *embonpoint* [actually she was five months gone with Nelson's child]. . . . Lord Nelson is a little man, without any dignity. Lady Hamilton takes possession of him, and he is a willing captive – the most submissive and devoted I have seen. Sir William is old, infirm, all admiration for his wife, and never spoke today but to applaud her.

Others thought that Emma looked like a barmaid, though Lady Malmesbury considered she behaved 'quite wonderfully, considering her origin and education'.

On arrival at Yarmouth the band played 'See the Conquering Hero Come' in the pouring rain, but in London their reception was cool. Nelson was snubbed at a royal levée and the attitude adopted by Fanny and Nelson's father may be imagined. The Hamiltons took a house at 23 Piccadilly and the Nelsons at 17 Dover Street near by. During the next few weeks he saw Emma every day, combining official functions, such as taking his seat in the House of Lords, or attending the Lord Mayor's banquet in his honour (the mob dragging his carriage up Ludgate Hill to Guildhall), with the painful and inevitable consequences of his affair with Emma.

The crisis was resolved in the first cruel weeks of the new year. On 3 January 1801, his oldest friend, Locker died. At breakfast a few days later he was going on in his usual style about Emma when Lady Nelson rose from the table. 'I am sick of hearing of "dear Lady Hamilton", and am resolved that you shall give up either her or me!' She left the room and it is doubtful if he ever saw her again.

It does not seem, however, as if the scene was intended to be final, and some doubt has been cast on the question whether it ever actually took place, though it rings true of a woman exasperated beyond endurance and Nelson's lawyer said that he had witnessed it. On 13 January he left London in order to join his new ship at Plymouth. At Southampton he wrote to Fanny : 'We are arrived, and heartily tired; and with the kindest regards to my father and all the family, believe me, your affectionate, Nelson.'

On his way west he called upon St Vincent, then living near Torquay. The old admiral reported on him to the Secretary of the Admiralty in the same terms as other naval officers at that time : 'Poor man! he is devoured with vanity, weakness and folly; was strung with ribbons, medals, etc., and yet pretended that he wished to avoid the honour and ceremonies he everywhere met with upon the road.'

At the end of the month there occurred the strangest scene of all in this sad story. Emma gave birth to a child, though no one suspected that such an event was probable because she had been entertaining on her usual scale right up to the last minute. What Nelson never knew was that it was not her first child : a girl by an earlier misalliance, named Emma Connor, was now nineteen years old. A few days after the birth of the new child, to be called Horatia, Emma arrived secretly at the house of a wet nurse called Mrs Gibson living in Marylebone. One story is that she had the baby concealed in her muff. Introducing herself as Lady Hamilton, she asked that the child should be brought at intervals to her house in Piccadilly. She demanded absolute discretion because, she said, she was acting on behalf of another lady who was the mother of the child and who promised handsome remuneration. It is possible that a second child was born to Emma and Nelson in 1804 but did not survive. All that Mrs Gibson was told was that the child's name was Horatia Thomson – the spelling varied in the cypher which the parents used when they wrote to each other on the subject. As she grew up, Horatia realized that she was Nelson's daughter, but she never accepted the fact that Emma was her mother, preferring Queen Carolina or some unnamed aristocratic lady.

Nelson heard of the birth of his child while his ship still lay in Torbay. He burned all Emma's letters. What is so strange is that it was not only the news about the child that exercised his mind during those days, but a frenzied attack of jealousy on hearing that so soon after the event Sir William (who seems to have known nothing about the birth, though it occurred in his own house) was asking the Prince Regent to dine at 23 Piccadilly. Knowing the Prince's reputation with women, Nelson wrote a series of apopletic notes to Emma – 'DO NOT let the lyar come. . . . May God Blast Him! Be firm! Go and dine with Mrs Denis on Sunday. Do not, I beseech you, risk being at home. Does Sir William want you to be a whore to the rascal?'

On 23 February he was granted a few days' leave in London before transferring his flag to the *St George* for the expedition to the Baltic. It seems cruel to reflect that about this time he and Emma must have seen Gillray's brutal caricature entitled 'Dido in Despair' (plate VI), which was published on 6 February, when it was known that he had gone to sea again. It depicts a female of monstrous size lamenting the departure of a fleet seen through the window of a room which is littered with bills and odd pieces of statuary. At the back an old man lies fast asleep.

What happened during those few days in London is not known. All that remains is the torn draft of a letter dated 4 March, which is endorsed by Lady Nelson: 'This is my Lord Nelson's letter of dismissal, which so astonished me that I immediately sent it to Mr Maurice Nelson, who was sincerely attached to me, for his advice; he desired me not to take the least notice of it, as his brother seemed to have forgot himself.' After telling her that he can do nothing more for Josiah, the letter concludes:

I neither want nor wish for any body to care what becomes of me, whether I return or am left in the Baltic, seeing I have done all in my power for you [i.e. settled £1,000 a year on her]. And if dead you will find I have done the same, therefore my only wish is to be left to myself and wishing you every happiness, believe that I am your affectionate Nelson and Brontë.

The turmoil aroused by these events helps to explain Nelson's impatience when he joined the fleet at Yarmouth. 'You, my beloved Emma, and my Country, are the two dearest objects of my fond heart', he wrote from his new flagship, and it is a measure of his greatness that for the next few months he could put the interests of his country above personal harassment. Indeed, he must have welcomed the prospect of active service as an escape from the domestic entanglements which he left behind when he sailed for the Baltic on 12 March 1801.

The importance of the Baltic to British shipping, and especially to the Royal Navy, had been increasing over the past century. As the native timber supply dwindled, and as the number and size of ships increased, overseas supplies of naval stores became vital. By this date Danzig plank, Riga masts, Stockholm tar, canvas, hemp, even copper and iron were all essential for the dockyards, whether private or royal. Hence it became a prime objective in British foreign policy to keep the Sound open to British shipping, and to deny such supplies to an enemy in time of war.

To achieve this, Britain had always insisted on the Right of Search of neutral shipping. Definitions of contraband were vague in the current state of international law, but the exercise of the right to stop and search neutrals was held by British lawyers to be 'an incontestable right of the lawfully commissioned cruisers of a belligerent power'. The practice was naturally resented by neutrals, and it inevitably led to conflict. In the recent American War of Independence the northern powers had formed an Armed Neutrality to protect their shipping. This had led to a declaration of war on the part of the Dutch and an indecisive battle fought off the Dogger Bank by Sir Hyde Parker.

Now, in 1801, another Armed Neutrality of the North was forming and another Hyde Parker (his son) was in command of an expedition to break it up. There had recently been trouble with Denmark (then united with Norway), when a Danish frigate had been captured after stiff resistance in the Channel and six vessels composing her convoy had been seized. Such insults to her flag compelled Denmark to take counsel with Russia, at that time ruled by the mad anglophobe Czar Paul. He had grievances of his own, because he had designs on Malta and wished to revive the Order of St John under his own patronage. When the French garrison there surrendered to the British after a long siege and the latter showed every sign of retaining the island for themselves, Paul lent a willing ear to proposals to revive the Armed Neutrality under his aegis. Napoleon, of course, fanned the flames, and Sweden and Prussia declared themselves anxious to join. These powers insisted (as the Americans have always insisted until they have become involved in a war) on the doctrine of Free Ships and Free Goods. They held that a declaration that a ship was not carrying contraband exempted her from the humiliation of an inspection of her cargo.

But matters did not stop there. Danish troops occupied the free cities of Lübeck and Hamburg and closed the Elbe to British shipping, and when the Russian government laid an embargo on British shipping in her northern ports and interned the crews, the Addington ministry decided that the time had come for a show of force. There was little mutual trust between the partners of the alliance, so it was hoped that the appearance of a strong British force in the Baltic would overawe the members of the alliance one by one; if not, a pre-emptive strike might be necessary.

Such was the general tenor of Parker's sailing orders. Their ambiguity was such as to deter a far more intelligent man than this ageing and unenterprising commander-in-chief, who had been put in command solely on account of his seniority. Talks with the Danish government were still pending when he sailed, so that it was explained that it remained uncertain if this temporizing policy 'should be terminated by an amicable agreement or by actual hostilities'. That was left to his judgment. In either case he was told to proceed to Reval (the modern Tallin at the mouth of the Gulf of Finland) as soon as ice permitted, 'and if he should find the division of the Russian navy usually stationed at that port still there, to make an immediate and vigorous attack upon it'. The first problem, however, was how to get there through the Sound if the fleets and forts on either side of it were hostile.

It was not only such a prospect that daunted Sir Hyde. It was also the embarrassing fact that a national hero has been sent to serve under him. Though the two men were on friendly, if distant, terms, it was like harnessing a race horse to a cart horse. As soon as Nelson joined he privately criticized the discipline of the fleet, its state of health and the obvious lack of enthusiasm on the part of the commander-in-chief for the service on which he was embarked. As he told St Vincent, 'Our friend is a little nervous about dark nights and fields of ice, but we must brace up; these are not times for nervous systems. I want Peace, which is only to be had through, I trust, our still invincible Navy.'

As soon as he could with decency press his ideas on Parker and outline a plan of campaign, he stressed the importance of immediate action. As a tactician, considerations of time were ever uppermost in his mind, as they have always been in the minds of the great masters of war. His impatience for speed on this occasion was borne out in the event. When the fleet passed the Sound it was fired on by a Danish fort at Kronborg (Elsinore) but not by the Swedes at Helsingborg on the opposite side, because that government had not yet made up its mind what action to take. Moreover, the Danish fleet at Copenhagen was hastily manned, a factor Nelson took into account when making the riskiest disposition of his ships which he ever made in his life.

The fleet destined for the Baltic was a very large one, but it had none of that cohesive strength which Nelson had known in the Mediterranean. Some of the ships had had the advantage of being trained under St Vincent, others were the scratch units normally designated for the North Sea fleet. It consisted of 2 three-deckers (Parker's *London* and Nelson's *St George*), 11 two-deckers, 7 slightly smaller 64-gun ships, and 6 frigates. Among Nelson's old friends were Foley, who had led the fleet at the battle of the Nile, now in the *Elephant*, to which Nelson transferred his flag when he needed a ship of shallower draft; Fremantle in the *Ganges*; Murray in the *Edgar*, who was to lead the fleet; and it was encouraging to see his old ship *Agamemnon* among the sixty-fours. Two notable officers he met for the first time were Captain Bligh of *Bounty* fame, who had shown at the battle of Camperdown what a doughty fighter he was and who was now to prove of invaluable service in the *Glatton*; and Edward Riou, captain of the frigate *Amazon*, on whose enterprise Nelson was to rely in all the preparations for the battle.

Nelson displayed his ability as a diplomatist as much as a sailor during the ensuing campaign. It was essential, in the first instance, to win the confidence of his commander-in-chief if he wished to enjoy a free hand. This he did in a well-accredited incident, though there have been some who have doubted it. Knowing Parker's partiality for good living, he rowed across to the flagship with the present of a freshly caught turbot. He was then, for the first time, invited to dine on board.

Embarrassed by the vaguenes of his instructions, Parker kept on holding councils of war. It was a habit which Nelson detested, because such councils were merely debates on the wider issues before the fleet; they were not the informal talks about the best way to engage the enemy which he himself favoured in the Mediterranean. After a long argument about whether it was wiser to proceed by the Belt or the Sound, he abruptly exclaimed 'I don't care a damn by which passage we go, so that we fight them.'

When at last they reached Copenhagen after making the passage by the Sound the enemy's position, hurriedly prepared as it was, seemed impregnable. The entrance to the harbour of the capital was not only protected by a citadel but by two formidable batteries erected on piles well out to sea called the Trekroner forts. From these forts the Danish fleet of 18 warships and a great many more armed hulks stretched southward in a line close to the shore for a distance of six kilometres (four miles). The ships were supposed to be supported by a line of batteries mounting 600 guns along the shore, though in the event the fire from these batteries was screened by the intervening ships. However, their gunners could easily be sent on board the ships as casualties increased.

More daunting than the Danish armament was the unbuoyed and uncharted approach to the capital known as the King's Channel, in which the enemy fleet was moored. This was a long, narrow channel running north and south between the shore and a wide shoal known as the Middle Ground, beyond which lay the main channel called the Outer Deep. Now that the buoys marking the limits of the shoal had been removed, its extent and bearings were unknown to the British as they moved down the Outer Deep to anchor at a point to the south of it, some three kilometres (two miles) from the southern end of the enemy line. It was obviously too hazardous to employ three-decked ships in such waters, so Nelson tansferred his flag to the *Elephant*. He told Parker that he could do the business if he was given ten such ships. Parker gave him twelve, together with Riou's frigates which, with their shallower draft, could pilot the way. With the remainder of the fleet Parker proposed to sail back along the Outer Deep in order to take up a position blocking the King's Channel's northern entrance, while Nelson's attacking force entered by the southern entrance.

A northerly wind was blowing when the fleet anchored on 1 April. The whole plan depended on a charge of wind to the opposite quarter the next day. What was also required was a far more accurate knowledge of the bearings of the Middle Ground. Riou, Hardy and others were sent out in boats all night to survey the entrance of the Channel, while Nelson planned detailed orders as to where each ship was to bring up when battle was joined.

Compared with the spontaneous and unrehearsed tactics employed at the Nile, the planning of the battle of Copenhagen was a masterpiece of careful foresight. On both occasions the enemy fleet lay at anchor, but this time it was impossible to get inside them because they lay so close to the shore. However, once again the tactics of concentrating on the van and working towards the centre were adopted. There was clearly no opportunity for manoeuvring: it was to be downright fighting against superior numbers but, in Nelson's judgment, inferior experience. All that could be done was to give each captain detailed instructions, and to inspire him with confidence.

It was in this respect that Nelson's genius as a leader was paramount. In Southey's words, 'he could electrify all within his atmosphere'. Or, as St Vincent put it (and he was not a man given to flattery), 'I never saw a man in our profession excepting yourself and Troubridge, who possessed the magic art of infusing the same spirit into others which inspired their own actions.' We are told that the night before the battle he invited all his captains to dinner on board the *Elephant*. 'He was in the highest spirits, and drank to a leading wind and to the success of the ensuing day.' They left for their respective ships full of confidence as to the outcome, while their admiral settled down to draft their orders. After a while Tom Allen, his servant, persuaded him to lie down instead of striding to and fro across the cabin, but even from his cot he kept on telling the copying clerks to hurry their work as reports came in that the wind was turning fair.

The work was finished at six o'clock in the morning, some time after Nelson had dressed and breakfasted. A signal was made for all captains to receive their orders at eight, Riou alone being told to act as circumstances might require. He was to lead the fleet in the *Amazon* and then take his frigates up to the end of the line opposite the Trekroner forts. The text of each captain's orders is too long to be quoted in full, but the general aim was for the leading ships to leapfrog each other until both the flagships, *Elephant* and *Dannebrog*, were engaged. The opening paragraphs are as follows :

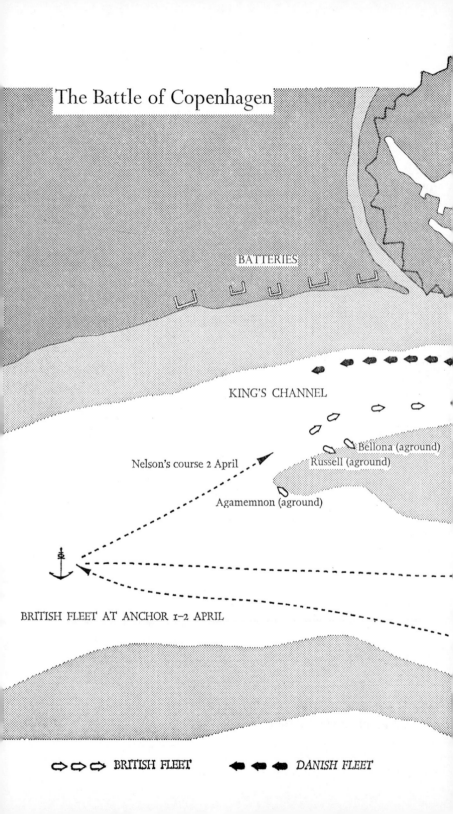

The Battle of Copenhagen

BATTERIES

KING'S CHANNEL

Nelson's course 2 April

Bellona (aground)

Russell (aground)

Agamemnon (aground)

BRITISH FLEET AT ANCHOR 1–2 APRIL

⇔ ⇔ ⇔ BRITISH FLEET   ◄ ◄ ◄ DANISH FLEET

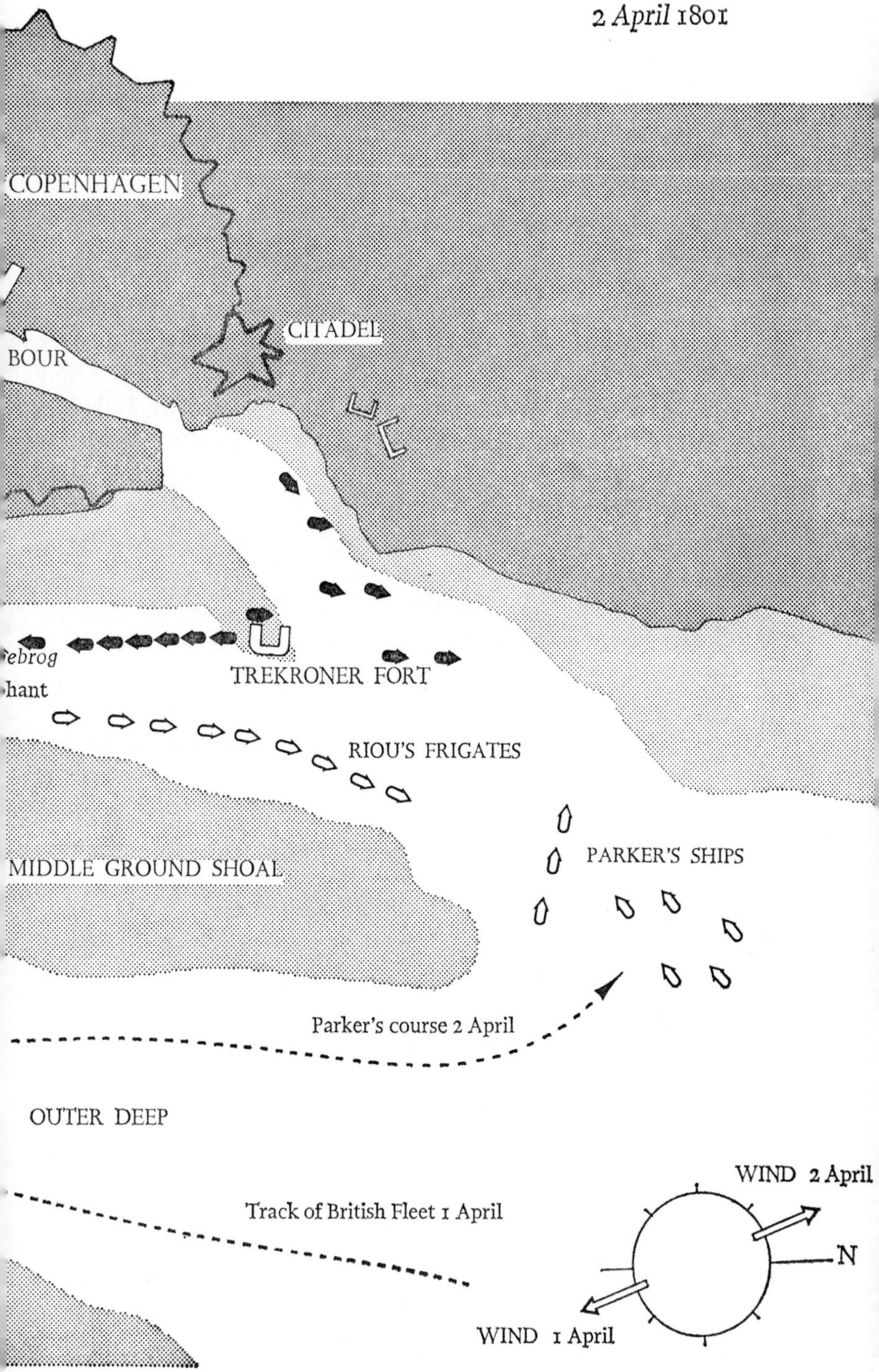

2 *April* 1801

COPENHAGEN

CITADEL

BOUR

TREKRONER FORT

ebrog
hant

RIOU'S FRIGATES

MIDDLE GROUND SHOAL

PARKER'S SHIPS

Parker's course 2 April

OUTER DEEP

Track of British Fleet 1 April

WIND 2 April

N

WIND 1 April

These ships are to fire in passing to their stations – *Edgar*, *Ardent*, *Glatton*, *Isis*, *Agamemnon* – and to lead in succession. The *Edgar* is to anchor abreast of No. 5. The *Ardent* is to pass the *Edgar* and anchor abreast of Nos. 6 and 7. The *Glatton* to pass the *Ardent* and anchor abreast of No. 9. The *Isis* to anchor abreast of No. 2. The *Agamemnon* to anchor abreast of No. 1. . . .

No word was spoken aboard the ships as they got under way except the chantings of the pilots and the helmsmen. The *Edgar* and *Ardent* were soon in their appropriate positions, followed by the *Glatton*, which engaged the *Dannebrog* with carronades at a very close range until the *Elephant* came up. However carefully the plans were made there were bound to be accidents in such shoal waters. First of all the *Agamemnon* failed to weather the southern tip of the Middle Ground. Soon afterwards the *Bellona* and *Russell* ran aground. Nelson's striking force of 12 ships was reduced to 9, but for the next four hours those nine battleships sustained a rate of fire such as had never been known for such a long time.

At the height of the action there occurred the famous incident of the blind eye. Just as Colonel Drinkwater has left us the best account of Nelson's first battle, so Colonel The Honourable William Stewart provided the most authentic account of the battle of Copenhagen, and he had the added advantage of being on the quarterdeck of the flagship throughout the action. He was there in command of 860 soldiers, half of them from the Rifle Corps, in case a landing should prove necessary. The story of the blind eye is best told in his own words :

A shot through the mainmast knocked a few splinters about us. He observed to me, with a smile, 'It is warm work, and this day may be the last of any of us at a moment'; and then stopping short at the gangway, he used an expression never to be erased from my memory, and said with emotion, 'but mark you, I would not be elsewhere for thousands'. When the signal, No. 39, was made the Signal Lieutenant reported to him. He continued his walk and did not appear to take notice of it. The Lieutenant meeting his Lordship at the next turn asked 'whether he should repeat it'. Lord Nelson answered, 'No, acknowledge it.' On the officer returning to the poop, his Lordship called after him, 'Is No. 16 still hoisted?' The Lieutenant answering in the affirmative, Lord Nelson said, 'Mind you keep it so.' He now walked the deck considerably agitated, which was always known by his moving the stump of his right arm. After a turn or two, he said to me, in a quick manner, 'Do you know what's shown on board the Commander-in-Chief, No. 39?' on asking him what that meant, he answered, 'Why "leave off action". Leave off action!' he repeated, and then added, with a shrug, 'Now, damn me if I do.' He also observed, I believe to Captain Foley, 'You know, Foley, I have only one eye – I have a right to be blind sometimes'; and then with an archness peculiar to his character, putting the glass to his blind eye, he exclaimed, 'I really do not see the signal.'

Parker made the signal with the best intentions. He thought that 'the fire was too hot for Nelson to oppose', so he judged that this signal would give him an excuse to break off action if he thought it necessary. Such niceties could not be expressed in a signal which was necessarily less permissive than the commander-in-chief intended. Riou, however, obeyed, with fatal consequences. As he turned towards Parker, the stern of the *Amazon* was exposed to battery fire. The ship was raked and the gallant Riou, one of the best officers in the Navy, was cut in two by shot.

By this time the enemy fire was slackening, though many of the gunners from the shore batteries had been brought on board to replace casualties. The *Dannebrog* was obviously out of control. She blew up, like *L'Orient*, at 4.30. Hostilities had never been formally declared, so that Nelson was unwilling to massacre a defeated fleet : the Danes were not Frenchmen. While the battle was still raging he sent a note under a flag of truce addressed

To the Brothers of Englishmen, the Danes. Lord Nelson has directions to spare Denmark, when no longer resisting; but if the firing is continued on the part of Denmark, Lord Nelson will be obliged to set on fire all the floating batteries he has taken, without having the power of saving the brave Danes who have defended them.

Some enthusiastic Danes took this to be a sign of defeat. The note was certainly sent at a critical moment for the British, whose rigging was so badly cut up that they would have been unable to escape even if they had wanted to. But when a lull in the battle was ended by more desultory firing on the part of the Danes, Nelson sent another note, this time addressed to the Danish government:

To the Government of Denmark. Lord Nelson's object in sending on shore a flag of truce is humanity: he therefore consents that hostilities should cease till Lord Nelson can take his prisoners out of the prizes, and he consents to land all the wounded Danes, and to burn or remove all his prizes.

There was no note of capitulation here. All firing ceased and the total of casualties was assessed. They were much heavier than usual in a sea battle – 941 on the British side, about 1,700 on the Danish. Yet this was the only battle in which Nelson himself suffered no injury. At 9 o'clock that night, 'very tired after a hard fought battle', he wrote a line to Emma and then threw himself exhausted on his cot.

The best comment on the action, said to be the hottest of the whole war, comes from Rear-Admiral Graves, his second-in-command: 'Considering the disadvantages of navigation, the approach to the enemy, their vast number of guns and mortars both on land and sea, I do not think there was ever a bolder attack. . . . In short, it was worthy of our gallant and enterprising little Hero of the Nile. Nothing can exceed his spirit.'

The next day Nelson landed to arrange an armistice with the Prince Royal, who acted as regent in place of his mentally afflicted father. A detailed account of this conversation was sent by Nelson to the Prime Minister. It is a good example of diplomatic bargaining which one would not have expected from a man of Nelson's impatient temperament, flushed as he was by such a notable victory. He was at pains to show that no hostility was intended between the two governments and he pretended that the battle (from the scene of which the Prince could still see smoke arising) was a demonstration against Denmark's

alliance with Russia. The Prince protested against such an in-
genuous view: in his eyes, Parker had declared war. 'This I
denied, and requested his Royal Highness to send for the papers.'
The Prince wisely side-stepped the issue by explaining his government's intentions to detach Denmark from the alliance.
Nelson then spoke in most undiplomatic terms about 'this freedom and nonsense of navigation', making it quite clear that
Britain would never abjure the Right of Search, and arguing
that it would be in Denmark's best interest to ally herself with
his country. 'Then Russia will go to war with us', the Prince
interjected. 'I told him he knew the offer of Great Britain, either
to join us, or disarm.' 'I pray, Lord Nelson, what do you call dis-
arming?' Nelson replied that he was not authorized to discuss
the subject, but the conditions for an armistice were the free
entry of the fleet into Copenhagen and the use of its port facili-
ties. 'Before I could go on, he replied "That you shall have with
pleasure".' On the question of relations with Russia, the Prince
refused to commit himself.

An armistice was therefore concluded on these lines. Nelson's demand for its duration to last sixteen weeks, in order to
have time to deal with the Russians and then return to Copenhagen, was whittled down to fourteen, but otherwise he was
quite justified in telling the Prime Minister that 'A negotiator is
certainly out of my line, but being thrown into it, I have en-
deavoured to acquit myself as well as I was able.' And Addington, when he moved a vote of thanks in the House of Commons
to the officers and seamen of the Northern Fleet, happily observed 'that Lord Nelson had shown himself as wise as he was
brave, and proved that there may be united in the same person
the talents of the Warrior and the Statesman'.

Nelson sailed on 12 April, Parker having already taken the
fleet a few kilometres south of Copenhagen to Kioge Bay. Their
intention was to proceed, as instructed, to Reval to deal with the
Russian squadron, or (as Nelson put it) to cut off the trunk of the
tree, the other members of the alliance thereby falling off of
their own accord. Once more he was exasperated at Parker's
dilatoriness in his impatience to get at the enemy. But this move

– as was the battle itself – had already been rendered unnecessary
by the fact that the Czar was strangled in a palace revolution on
24 March. It is extraordinary to us that the news should have
taken so long to become public, but, as we know, the Russians
are a secretive people, and it was long ago pointed out that their
constitution was (as it continues to be) absolutism moderated by
assassination.

Colonel Stewart had been sent home with despatches. He
returned to the Baltic a month later with fresh instructions.
What surprised the fleet was that among these orders was the
abrupt recall of Sir Hyde Parker, whose place was to be taken
by Nelson, now created a Viscount for his services. Many regarded Parker's dismissal as an insult to the fleet, and all (including Nelson) thought the idea of an enquiry into his
behaviour most ill-advised. Naval officers knew from history the
dangerous consequences of such enquiries or courts martial:
within living memory the Keppel–Pallisser affair had split the
fleet. 'His friends in the fleet', wrote Nelson privately, 'wish
everything of this fleet to be forgot, for we all respect and love
Sir Hyde; but the dearer his friends, the more uneasy they have
been at his *idleness*, for that is the truth – no criminality.'

The new orders Nelson was instructed to carry out were
to suspend hostilities with Russia, but to enquire at Reval
whether the embargo on British ships had been taken off and
their crews released. It was typical, says Stewart, that the first
signal made by the new commander-in-chief on 7 May was to
prepare to weigh. Having reached Reval it was found that the
Russian squadron had left for Cronstadt a few days earlier. Since
the position of Sweden remained equivocal, Nelson wrote to the
Swedish admiral advising him to keep his fleet in port to avoid
any occasion for hostilities. Friendly relations were soon established between both powers, so that Nelson could leave the Gulf
of Finland to return to Denmark. It is worth adding that a similar
situation arose out of the insoluble problem of the Right of
Search v. Free Ships and Free Goods in 1807, when the city of
Copenhagen was burned and its fleet cut out by Lord Gambier in
order to detach it from another coalition against Britain.

Nelson had been demanding his recall for sometime. 'Why am I to be kept here to die a natural death?' he asked his agent, Alexander Davison, 'I did not bargain for that when I came to the Baltic.' There were good reasons for his impatience to get home. Having spent most of his life in the Mediterranean or in tropical climates, the cold of a Baltic spring did not suit him, so that he suffered from what sounds like psychosomatic stomach pains. For a fortnight he was confined to his bed, as was his second in command. He felt that his work was done, and he was never one for hanging about awaiting fresh instructions. As his friend Stewart put it, 'his health was not good, and his mind was not at ease', chiefly because he longed to see Emma and his child again. Having performed great services to the state, there was no longer any reason why he should not return to private life once more.

At the end of May St Vincent (now First Lord of the Admiralty) agreed to his repeated requests to be superseded. On 1 July he landed at Yarmouth, and it is typical of his loyalty to the service and of his humanity that his first action, before taking the coach to London and Emma, was to visit the naval hospital there to enquire after those who had been wounded in the battle, and to give each of the nurses a guinea.

8 On the Beach

It was about this time that Nelson assumed the image with which posterity is familiar. He was now forty-three years old, still the small, slight figure he was when Rigaud first painted him as a junior officer. This, his most attractive portrait (plate I), was superseded by the more popular portrait done by Lemuel Abbott in 1797, when he was recovering from the loss of his arm. Many later versions of this exist, as well as a host of engravings which made his appearance familiar throughout the land. It shows the hair whiter than the sandy-grey of other pictures, the blank look in the right eye, the empty sleeve pinned across his chest. It is a highly idealized image, but it suited the taste of a romantic age which Nelson's personality and career so perfectly expressed.

A portrait by Sir William Beechey done after his return from the Baltic gives a better idea of the vitality of the man, especially in the sketch (plate V) rather than the finished version. More conventional is the full-length portrait by Hoppner (see plate VII for a sketch for this), which seems to exaggerate the height of a man who was only 5 foot 4 inches tall. Anyone who looks at the uniform coats in the National Maritime Museum realizes what a small man he was. By far the most realistic portrayal is the effigy in Westminster Abbey (jacket illustration) based by Catharine Andras on the Hoppner portrait soon after Nelson's death, though he sat for her earlier on. The plasticity of the wax models the contours of his face, giving it a strikingly life-like appearance, 'as though he was standing there', as the Duchess of Devonshire said.

Nelson was not a handsome nor a dignified man, in the

accepted meaning of those words. What impressed everyone who met him was the intense vitality in his fragile frame, the eager manner and simple, open address. This is what fascinated new acquaintances and what electrified those who served under him. The many tributes to his singular power to charm which are made by subordinates are unusually frank because, as his secretary said, he was 'so cheerful and pleasant that it was a happiness to be about his hand'. It was thus not only his record as a victorious admiral which made men love to serve under him. When his barge crew, for example, wished to accompany him back to England they expressed the hero-worship combined with personal affection which he seems to have invariably inspired: 'My lord, It is with extreme grief that we find you are about to leave us. . . . My lord, pardon the rude style of seamen who are but little acquainted with writing, and believe us to be, my Lord, your most humble and obedient servants. Barge's crew of the *Foudroyant*.'

Such men were not affected by what many people find repellent about some aspects of his character. The miserable business in the Bay of Naples, the vanity and silliness of those years, the blatant xenophobia, are not part of that indefinable 'Nelson Touch' which the mob on shore loved as much as the men at sea. He basked in his popularity, which seemed to give him renewed strength when he was depressed. His histrionic style is reflected in the design of his career, which moves to a dramatic climax like a theatrical performance.

The contrast between Nelson the naval hero and Wellington the military hero is inescapable: a contrast between the voluble and the reticent, the man who loved the mob and achieved the noblest death, and the man who stood so aloof from its plaudits that it broke his windows after he had failed to be killed at the summit of his career. The contrast is vividly illustrated at their one meeting in Whitehall on 12 September 1805. Sir Arthur Wellesley, as he then was, had no pretensions to fame at that date: he was a sepoy general just back from India, whereas Nelson was at the climax of his popularity. Many years later the Duke recorded the interview in these words:

I went to the Colonial Office in Downing Street, and there I was shown into the little waiting room on the right hand, where I found a gentleman whom, from his likeness to his picture and the loss of an arm, I immediately recognised as Lord Nelson. He could not know who I was, but he entered at once into conversation with me, if I can call it conversation, for it was almost all on his side, and all about himself; and in, really, a style so vain and silly as to surprise and almost disgust me. I suppose something that I happened to say may have made him guess that I was somebody, and he went out of the room for a moment, I have no doubt to ask the office-keeper who I was, for when he came back he was altogether a different man, both in manner and matter. All that I thought a charlatan style had vanished, and he talked of the state of this country and of the aspect and probabilities of affairs on the Continent with a good sense and a knowledge of subjects both at home and abroad that surprised me equally and more agreeably than the first part of our interview had done: in fact, he talked like an officer and a statesman. . . . I saw enough to be satisfied that he was really a very superior man; but certainly a more sudden and complete metamorphosis I never saw.

There was certainly no trace of the traditional Silent Service about Nelson at this or any other time. The contrast would seem to be between the Anglo-Saxon and the Celt. As Bernard Shaw pointed out, 'the contrast is English against Irish all over, and is the more delicious because the real Irishman in it (Wellington) is the Englishman of tradition, whilst the real Englishman (Nelson) is the traditional theatrical foreigner'. In the preface to *John Bull's Other Island* Shaw compares, with his customary perverse paradoxes, the character of the Irish with the English. As usual, he cuts Nelson down to size by saying that 'he never had to fight a technically capable and properly equipped enemy except on land, where he had never been successful. Nelson, intensely nervous and theatrical, made an enormous fuss about victories so cheap that he would have deserved shooting if he had lost them' – the sort of remark which sounds so much more effective than it reads because, though it has a grain of truth in it, it ignores any serious examination of the balance of forces or the issues at stake. Southey was nearer the truth in portraying such a complex character when he said that 'the best eulogy of Nelson is the faithful history of his actions', something which St Vincent told him after the battle of Copenhagen: 'Your Lordship's whole conduct, from your first appointment to this hour, is the subject of our constant admiration: it does not become me to make comparisons; all agree there is but one Nelson.'

Such being the case, he was soon employed again. In February 1801, the peace of Lunéville was signed between France and Austria. As after the collapse of the First Coalition, Britain remained the only enemy and Bonaparte had to revive the old plans for an invasion of the British Isles with an army said to be 40,000 strong. For the first time both he and Nelson took the plan seriously, though Nelson could never imagine how so large a force could be embarked at Boulogne on account of the tides; he thought Flushing more likely.

His appointment was to the Downs command, stretching from Beachy Head in Sussex to Orfordness in Suffolk, with Deal as headquarters. The channel between the coast and the Goodwin Sands known as the Downs was the principal route for shipping approaching the Thames, but it was not so much the defence of shipping as the embarrassment of the enemy flotilla across the straits of Dover which concerned Nelson. 'The whole of this business', he told the Duke of Clarence, 'is of no further moment than to show the enemy that, with impunity, they cannot come outside their ports', because 'our first defence is close to the enemy's ports.' Such has ever been the doctrine of offensive strategists from the time of Drake. As for the defence of the coast itself, he wrote to the Admiralty in Churchillian vein that 'the moment the enemy touch our coast, be it where it may be, they are to be attacked by every man afloat or on shore; this must be perfectly understood. Never fear the event'.

The pattern of the strategy for the defence of the British Isles which was to be enforced by his successors at a later stage of the war was by now fully evolved. St Vincent had taught the Channel Fleet that its task was the close blockade of Brest. The lines of defence at the most vulnerable parts of the Downs and the Nore were composed of a flotilla of light craft cruising off

the enemy coast, backed by a second line of coastal craft sup-
posedly manned by Sea Fencibles, a type of naval militia or
reserve which came into existence at this time. On land, Mar-
tello Towers – strongpoints adopted after experience of their
use in Corsica – were built along the coast, where the regular
Army, supplemented by local volunteer forces, was responsible
for any actual landing.

It was not the sort of task that suited Nelson's temperament or his talents. He never had the patience for the dull
routine of close blockade and he would much have preferred
the more senior command in the Mediterranean. Though his
tour of duty only lasted during the summer months, he was constantly cold and seasick, complaining of toothache and stomach
troubles and obviously not fully recovered from the illness
which he suffered in the Baltic. But in the early summer, at least,
he threw himself into the task with his usual zeal, constantly
cruising off Boulogne in a frigate, or writing statesmanlike
papers on methods of defence.

As he soon came to realize, the trouble was that the country
was bored by a war which had already lasted nearly ten years.
The new scheme for raising Sea Fencibles for coastal defence
attracted plenty of gentleman volunteers but few fishermen.
This led him to write a paper on manning in which he pro-
pounded a plan 'to make our seamen, at the din of war, fly to
our Navy, instead of flying from it'. The plan was no more
practical than any one of the hundreds put forward in the past
to solve an intractable problem. The merchant marine was supposed to provide a pool of seamen for the Navy in a war; but as
he had discovered while still a midshipman, a merchant seaman,
especially at this stage of the war, would do anything to avoid
impressment, or desert at the first opportunity. Nelson thought
that if a man serving in the Navy was given a certificate of good
conduct, if his prize money was paid promptly, if his pay was
supplemented by two guineas annually and four guineas for
every eight years' service, the Navy would become an attractive career. It was not to be. Not until a regular long-service
Navy came into existence in the middle of the nineteenth cen-

tury did the old hire-and-discharge, hand-to-mouth methods of manning disappear; even then, as we have seen in the last two wars, conscription (which is the same thing as impressment by politer means) became inevitable when the armed services needed to expand to any great extent.

Nelson had under his command in the Downs 57 vessels of the smaller type – frigates, brigs, cutters. He was determined to do something with them in addition to their normal cruising duties. A grand cutting-out expedition at Boulogne was planned for the night of 15 August. The optimism with which he launched the plan – 'our folks have only to go on, never think of retiring' – did not augur well for its success, if one recalls what happened at Teneriffe. This time he did not lead the boats in person, for which he reproached himself afterwards. The boats became separated in the darkness. They arrived singly to find themselves under heavy fire from the shore by mortars and musketry and, what was worse, to discover that the French flat-bottomed barges were not secured by ropes but by chains. After suffering heavy casualties, they retired without accomplishing anything.

Rumours of peace were becoming stronger, the preliminaries of the Treaty of Amiens being signed that autumn. Nelson immediately applied for leave, which was granted, though he did not actually haul down his flag until the terms were ratified in April 1802. One may sympathize with his disgust at the concessions made by this absurd treaty. Admiral Lord Keith and General Sir Ralph Abercromby had completed his victory at the Nile by defeating the French army in Egypt, but the enemy were permitted to reembark for France on exactly the same terms as had been offered years before by the Convention of El Arish, which Britain had foolishly abrogated. It was intended to hand back Malta (for which Nelson never had much use) to the Knights of St John, though it had been in British hands for some time. All overseas conquests, including the Cape of Good Hope, with the exception of Ceylon and Trinidad, were restored – Martinique, Guadaloupe, even Minorca, the only base for a Mediterranean fleet. We need not enquire why the Addington government imagined that Bonaparte, now First Consul, would keep his part of the bargain to wind up the Batavian and Helvetic republics and to evacuate Italy. Yet even St Vincent, now First Lord, thought that he would, and with his passion for economy proceeded to dismantle the Navy which had been built up so laboriously over so many years. He thought the peace would last. Nelson doubted it, but at least an armistice would give him a most welcome and much needed respite for himself.

Before he went on leave he had asked Emma to find some convenient home for retirement. That autumn Merton Place, 'the farm' as Nelson called it, was purchased. It was a pleasant country house in Surrey with a large garden and a stream, which of course Emma called the Nile. It was within easy reach of London, yet conveniently outside the haunts of London society which had cold-shouldered Emma in Piccadilly. Horatia could be brought for short visits and it was ideal for the recuperation of Nelson's health.

Emma furnished it and entertained there with her usual extravagance, though neither Sir William nor Nelson was a rich man. A balance sheet which he drew up at this time shows that his net income was only £768 a year. Whereas St Vincent and Duncan had been voted a pension of £3,000 for each of their victories, Nelson was only given £2,000 for two, and virtually a third. For the loss of his eye and his arm he received a naval pension of £923. His half-pay as Vice-Admiral amounted to a mere £465. Out of this he paid an allowance of £1,800 to Fanny and £350 to his brother's widow and his nephews. Taking debts into account, he reckoned that his expenditure was £2,650 and his income £3,418.

A pathetic attempt was made at this time by Fanny to regain her husband's affections. Writing from her retirement at Bath, she congratulates him on his victory at Copenhagen and concludes

Let me beg, nay intreat you to believe no Wife ever felt greater affection for a Husband than I do, and to the best of my knowledge I have invariably done everything you desire. . . . Do, my dear husband, let us live together. I can never be happy till such an event

VI 'Dido in Despair' – cartoon by Gillray, 1801

VII   Nelson in 1802 – oil sketch by John Hoppner

takes place. I assure you that I have but one wish in the world, to please you. Let every thing be buried in oblivion, it will pass away like a dream. I can now only intreat you to believe I am most sincerely and affectionately your wife.

The letter bears the inscription 'Opened by mistake, but not read'.

Unquestionably, the spring and summer of 1802 was one of the happiest times of his life. A tour of the West Country and South Wales which he and Emma took that summer was a fine holiday and the acclamations he met with at every place restored his spirits. He occasionally visited London to speak in the House of Lords, much to the alarm of Hardy, who said 'I am sorry for it, and I am fully convinced that sailors should not talk too much'. But he avoided the town as much as possible. As he told St Vincent, 'Large dinners truly alarm me.'

About one such dinner a pleasant anecdote survives. He was sitting next to Benjamin West, and praising his 'Death of Wolfe' painting, since it had obvious attractions for him. Why had West not done more like it? 'Because, my Lord, there are no more subjects.' 'Damn it,' replied Nelson, 'I didn't think of that!' 'But, my Lord,' continued the artist, 'I fear that your intrepidity may yet furnish me with another such scene, and if it should I shall certainly avail myself of it.' 'Will you?' asked Nelson eagerly, pouring out a glass of champagne, 'Will you, Mr West? Then I hope I shall die in the next battle.' West was to paint a 'Death of Nelson' and also two sentimental versions of an apotheosis, one in oils and one in Code stone on a pediment at what was then the Royal Hospital, Greenwich. It was there, in the Painted Hall, that Nelson's body was to lie in state and many of his portraits and relics were to be preserved for the next hundred years.

Lord Minto (whom Nelson first met as Sir George Elliot) describes the household at Merton as if it was at Naples:

She is in high looks, but more immense than ever. She goes on cramming Nelson with trowelfuls of flattery, which he goes on taking as quietly as a child does pap.

The whole house was a Nelson museum, with portraits, mementoes and trophies all over the place. Though Nelson was happy in such surroundings, it is doubtful if Sir William was. He was now an old man who had sold his collection and wanted nothing more than a quiet life, the last thing that Emma could provide. He grumbled about 'the nonsense I am obliged to submit to here to avoid coming to an explosion which would be attended by many disagreeable effects, and would totally disturb and destroy the comfort of the best man and best friend I have in the world'. In the last note which he wrote to his wife he admits that when he married her he expected to be 'superannuated', but as their tastes differed all that he now asked was that 'the very silly altercations that happen but too often between us and embitter the present moments exceedingly' should cease and that she should allow him to pass the evening of his life according to his own inclinations.

There is no time for nonsense or trifling. I know and admire your talents, and many excellent qualities, but I am not blind to your defects and confess having many myself; therefore let us bear and forebear for God's sake.

Three months later on 6 April 1803, he died. In his will he left an enamel picture of Emma 'to my dearest friend, Lord Nelson, Duke of Brontë; a very small token of the great regard I have for his Lordship, the most virtuous, loyal and truly brave character I ever met with. God bless him, and shame fall on those who do not say "Amen".'

So ended the extraordinary *ménage à trois*. Only six weeks later war with France was renewed. On 18 May, two days after it was declared, Nelson hoisted his flag on board the *Victory* at Spithead.

9 The Campaign of Trafalgar

The war which was resumed in 1803 lasted ten years after Nelson's death. During its latter stages, when Napoleon controlled most of the continent of Europe, it became the classic example of the conflict between land and sea power, but before the victory of Trafalgar gave Britain supremacy at sea its character was that of a duel between two nations fought out by an army with still undefeated fleets on the one side and a greatly superior naval force standing on the defensive on the other. It was only in the spring of 1805 that Britain moved to a diplomatic and to a lesser degree a military offensive. Until a few months before Nelson's death, the point at issue was the success or failure of Napoleon's plans to invade the British Isles.

During those years Napoleon (calling himself First Consul until his coronation as Emperor in 1805) was building up the Grand Army on the north-east coast of France in camps at Etaples, Boulogne, Wimereux, Calais and Dunkirk. He hoped to achieve an army of 150,000 men, but by the summer of 1805 there were only 93,000 ready to cross the Channel in 1,928 boats – 130-foot long *prames*, *bâteaux plats*, and such transport craft. In his opinion, he could embark this great force on two or three tides, but to British observers this was an impossible task requiring a much longer period and perfect weather. 'Let us be masters of the straits for six hours and we shall be masters of the world', he exclaimed at his most optimistic. 'I don't say the French can't come', was St Vincent's reply, 'I say they can't come by sea.' All previous attempts at invasion had failed, so that the country, now thoroughly aroused by the threat, was confident that it could repel any landing – even if the King took

command of the troops, as he threatened to do. Without appre-
ciating the strength of the disposition of naval forces, the ordinary citizen was content to know that Nelson was at sea, and
that with his record the maritime danger was negligible. So
when, in the opening stage of the Trafalgar campaign, it seemed
as if Nelson had lost control of the situation, the alarm was all
the more pronounced.

In later years Napoleon pretended, on occasion, that he
never intended to invade Britain at all. The whole business was
to be regarded as a gigantic bluff for the purpose of putting
Britain on the defensive. His correspondence at the time, however, lends no colour to this excuse for failure. It is true that he
was constantly changing his plans and the methods by which
his objectives were to be attained. At the end of 1804 he seems to
have lost faith for a while in the whole project, but the declaration of war against Britain by Spain at that moment provided him with another 32 sail of the line. Once more he changed
his plans in favour of a grand diversionary design which brought
into play the great number of ships he now had at his disposal
just when events seemed to be taking a more favourable turn
in his direction.

During the brief period of the Peace of Amiens the Royal
Navy was largely dismantled and most of its ships laid up 'in
ordinary'. As soon as war broke out again, and especially when
Pitt resumed power with Melville (Dundas) as his First Lord of
the Admiralty, there was a rapid expansion. Whereas in 1803
there were only 32 ships of the line in commission, in 1805
there were 181. The List of Ships in Commission for July gives
a total of 570 ships and 117,304 men in sea pay. To this force
must be added the Sea Fencibles, the Militia, the local defence
Volunteers and a regular Army of 85,000 men, out of a total
population of England and Wales of about 8 million.

The distribution of forces at sea followed the traditional
strategic pattern for a defensive war. Nelson's old command in
the Downs was given to Keith, who, as Commander-in-Chief,
North Sea, now controlled shipping in the Thames and at Yarmouth, as well as the flotilla watching Boulogne in the Downs.

He was responsible for guarding the enemy coast from Le Havre to the Texel with 13 old ships of the line and a total of 113 smaller vessels. Characteristically, he was never in favour of dangerous enterprises, though he was persuaded to allow trial of two unorthodox forms of warfare – Congreve's incendiary rockets fired from boats ('the soul of artillery without the body', as the inventor put it), and Fulton's torpedoes, 18-foot copper cylinders, variously named 'carcasses', 'catamarans' or 'curiosities', which were towed into position before the clockwork mechanism was set off. The American inventor, now living in England under the name of 'Francis', had recently submerged the *Nautilus* in the Seine as the first submarine, but over here he confined himself to explosive mines which he was the first to call 'torpedoes'. Rockets continued to be used by sea and land, but after Fulton's return to the United States there was little development of the torpedo, which was generally disapproved of as a weapon of warfare unfit for civilized nations.

Linking Keith's force at one end of the Channel with the much larger force blockading Brest was a squadron under Saumarez based on his native Channel Islands, the chief use of which was to obtain information about the strength of the enemy by means of smugglers.

In command of the Channel Fleet of 35 sail of the line was the Honourable William Cornwallis, the senior admiral afloat, who was responsible for the blockade of Rochefort as well as the main fleet at Brest under Ganteaume. This was the hinge on which all British strategy turned. His orders to commanders of the inshore squadron of frigates illustrate the methods of Close Blockade which he inherited from St Vincent:

The strictest watch is to be kept on the port of Brest. The squadron with me will keep its station off Ushant as long as possible, but should it, by stress of weather, be forced to the eastward, the greatest care will be taken not to be driven beyond Torbay. And you are, with the ships under your orders, should it blow from the westward, to take shelter in Douarnenez Bay.

As St Vincent had proved, with the prevalent westerly wind it was impossible for the French to come out, and when it blew from the east it was equally difficult, provided the blockading force remained well up with Ushant. This was the central fact which Napoleon, accustomed as he was to moving armies independent of wind and weather, refused to accept. It was no use ordering Ganteaume to sea if the wind was contrary, nor to forbid him to fight an action if the British were just over the horizon. Hence the long and successful continuance of the British blockading fleet, nourished as it was by a chain of storeships from Plymouth and finding in Torbay a refuge when a south-westerly gale drove it off station. These were the distant, storm-beaten ships which, in Mahan's celebrated phrase, stood between the Grand Army and the dominion of the world.

When Spain entered the war a squadron of four ships was sent under Sir John Orde to watch Cadiz, but it was Nelson's task with the Mediterranean fleet of nine – later eleven – ships to control the whole of that sea from Cape St Vincent to Malta. Since Minorca had been restored to Spain by the peace treaty, Malta and Gibraltar were the only ports of refuge, and these lay too far from the scene of action. In order to watch Toulon he therefore used the anchorage at the Maddalena Islands, north-east of Sardinia, to provide security for his ships and much appreciated trips ashore for men on watering parties. When Emma threatened to join him on board, he wrote; 'Imagine what a cruise off Toulon is. Even in the summer we have a hard gale every week, and two days' heavy swell. It would kill you and myself to see you.'

With his eleven ships he had to watch an approximately equal force which was commanded by La Touche-Tréville until Villeneuve replaced him on his death in 1804. This Nelson did by methods quite different from those adopted by Cornwallis, that is to say by an Open Blockade, the object of which was to tempt the enemy out to sea rather than to shut him in. 'The port of Toulon has never been blockaded by me,' he once wrote, 'quite the reverse – every opportunity has been offered to the enemy to put to sea, for it is there we hope to realize the hopes and expectations of our country.' There was much to be said both for and against such tactics. Constant cruising kept his fleet healthy and alert, but it wore down the ships and a sudden change of weather might provide the enemy with more of an opportunity than Nelson allowed for in such a wide sea. Hence it was Villeneuve, not Ganteaume, who ultimately made good his escape.

When Nelson hoisted his flag on board the *Victory* to take up his command there was a conflict of emotion in his heart. The parting with Emma, just after Horatia's christening in secret and so soon after Sir William's death had set them free, was a cruel one. There is bitter pathos in the letter which he wrote to her as he left Spithead :

I feel from my soul that God is good, and in His due wisdom will unite us, only when you look upon our dear child call to re-membrance all you think I would say was I present, and be assured that I am thinking of you every moment. My heart is full to bursting.

On the other hand there was immense pride in assuming so senior a command in the finest three-decker afloat, famous in her own day and still visited annually by tens of thousands of people. From the *Victory*'s long and chequered history it is enough to say that, having been laid down in 1759, her age often threatened her with destruction. Recently she had a noble record, having borne the flags of Howe, Hood and St Vincent. Over 60 metres (200 feet) long and 2,000 tons burthen, she was (and is) a three-decker of 104 guns – thirty 32-pounders on the Lower Deck, twenty-eight 24-pounders on the Middle Deck, thirty 12-pounders on the Quarter Deck and two on the Fore-castle. In addition, she carried two 68-pound carronades on the Upper Deck for close action. The Great Cabin afforded every comfort the weather permitted. Champagne and claret were served regularly for dinner, with a rummer of punch at supper, but Nelson, being an abstemious man, was usually in bed by nine o'clock. Dr Beatty gives this description of his habits at this time :

He possessed a wonderful alacrity of mind, as even prevented him from taking ordinary repose, seldom enjoying two hours of uninterrupted sleep; and on several occasions he did not quit the deck the whole night. At these times he took no pains to protect himself from the wet, or the night air; wearing only a thin great coat; and he has frequently, after having his clothes wet through with rain, refused to have them changed, saying the leather waistcoat which he wore over his flannel one would secure him from complaint. He seldom wore boots, and was consequently very liable to have his feet wet. . . . There was slight rheumatic affection of the stump of his amputated arm on any sudden variation in the state of the weather. His Lordship usually predicted an alteration in the weather with as much certainty from feeling transient pains in his stump as he could by his marine barometer.

The Muster Book of the *Victory* for October 1805 shows that her complement was 837 men (nominally 850), of whom 628 composed 'the People'. There were then on board 3 sick, 31 Boys First Class (whom we should call officer cadets), 144 marines, 121 'supernumeraries' (officers of all sorts, including the admiral), 8 'widow's men' (a fictitious rating whose wages were allocated to the benefit of relatives) and 9 marked 'Run', i.e. deserted. Of the ship's company, only 319 men were pressed men, an unusually small proportion. They came from every county in the British Isles and they included 48 foreigners, of whom 23 were Americans, many were negroes and one was Swiss. The stations of the 745 men who were 'quartered' are shown in Appendix II.

The most remarkable feature about these figures is the small sick list. Nelson himself, and most of his men, was at sea without putting foot on shore for twenty months between May 1803 and July 1805. To have kept a fleet healthy and in a high state of morale for that length of time was an extraordinary achievement. With some pride, he told a doctor friend that while 'Cornwallis had great merit for his persevering cruise, he has everything sent him : we have nothing. We seem forgotten by the great folks at home. Our men's minds, however, are always kept up with daily hopes of meeting the enemy.' He claims that constant cruising between Barcelona, Tunis, Sardinia and Sicily kept his men on the alert. Plenty of onions, fresh meat and water maintained their health. Scurvy, which had hitherto been the bane of long periods at sea, was kept at bay by a liberal supply of lemon juice – 20,000 gallons of Sicilian juice at 1/6 a gallon being ordered in June 1804. Nothing gives a better idea of the complexity of maintaining and supplying a fleet at sea than a study of the accounts of the Agent Victuallers. That summer 505,047 pieces of beef were purchased, 379 sheep, 21,300 oranges, 61,685 lb onions, 119,015 gallons of wine, 30,326 of brandy. On such a diet, with the encouragement of diversions such as bands, amateur theatricals, with a new hospital at Malta, Nelson maintained his fleet for two years at a high standard of efficiency. With their long experience at sea, and under his leadership, his ships would be more than a match for any opponent; foul bottoms and the constant wear and tear of cordage and canvas were the only things they had to fear.

The English as well as the French government was on the offensive in 1805. Preliminary steps were taken when Pitt realized that another European Coalition might be fanned into existence. Russia and Austria had agreed on a defensive alliance before the end of the previous year, when Pitt made overtures to Russia. Progress towards such an alliance was blocked at first by the obstacle of Malta, which the Czar wanted and on which a British garrison still remained. Even Nelson came round to the view that it was 'the most important outwork to India' and might help to control the Levant. That spring, seven Russian sail of the line appeared in the eastern Mediterranean, so that Pitt despatched a token force of six battalions to Malta to act in conjunction with the Russians if necessary. This force, under Sir James Craig, sailed on 19 April, after being windbound for some time. To his fury, Nelson was not informed of its destination, so that during the ensuing chase of the French fleet he had to take into consideration the possibility of its being attacked as it crept down the western coast of the Iberian peninsula. Much needed ships had to be detached for its protection. When Napoleon heard that the force had sailed, he hailed it as yet another example of the English disdain for the strategical principle of the concentration of force. As he told the Minister of Marine,

If it is destined for Malta, so much the better. Nothing will prove more strongly the ineptitude of the English Cabinet; for these plans of continental operations based on detachments of a few thousand men are the plans of pygmies. If you hear that this expedition has gone to Malta, rejoice, for the English have deprived themselves of 6,000 men and a number of ships.

In the event, however, Craig's force achieved its object by sealing the Anglo-Russian alliance.

The first move in the development of the French offensive was made on 17 January, when Villeneuve escaped from Toulon with eleven ships while Nelson was off Sardinia. The latter sped east towards Alexandria, but the French course was westward until a gale forced them to put back on 21 January while Nelson was still in the neighbourhood of Malta. Missiessy, however, with the small Rochefort squadron carried out his orders to reach the West Indies.

The ease with which Villeneuve had escaped encouraged Napoleon to develop his grand diversionary design. In order to control the Channel for the passage of the Grand Army from Boulogne and neighbouring ports, he planned that both Ganteaume and Villeneuve should escape to the West Indies, the former picking up ships at Ferrol on his way, the latter joining Gravina's fleet at Cadiz. Once at Martinique, they were to wait thirty days for each other and after they were united in a force of forty big ships, they were to return to sweep away Cornwallis and enter the Channel. It was an admirable plan on paper, but success depended on a number of factors which Napoleon entirely overlooked. He imagined that Ganteaume could leave Brest as easily as Villeneuve did Toulon. 'A naval victory in existing circumstances can lead to nothing', he told him. 'Keep but one end in view – to fulfill your mission. Get to sea without an action.' He also omitted to take into account British naval strategy which, in brief, amounted to a concentration of all forces at the mouth of the Channel in the event of losing track of the enemy. 'The Western Squadron is the mainspring from which all offensive operations must proceed', wrote Lord Barham, now First Lord of the Admiralty.

In order to appreciate the movement of forces during the summer of 1805 it is necessary to bear in mind the slowness at which fleets moved under sail, and the absence of any reliable information about such movements on the part of both sides. Neither Nelson nor the Admiralty had, of course, any idea of what was in Napoleon's mind. Guesses as to what Villeneuve intended to do depended on scraps of rumour culled from neutral vessels, of which there were not many. When in doubt, the Admiralty favoured the strategy of falling back on Cornwallis: but, having already missed Villeneuve to his chagrin, Nelson was determined to bring him to action wherever it might be, even if it meant crossing the Atlantic with an inferior force. Many authorities have praised this decision, so typical of the offensive spirit; but it does seem that he was taking an enormous risk in imagining that he could find and fight the combined enemy fleets, which in the event returned to Europe unscathed. Had the Brest fleet by any chance also escaped, Nelson must have been overwhelmed by sheer weight of numbers in the West Indies.

On 30 March Villeneuve again escaped while Nelson was off Sardinia. On 9 April the French joined Gravina's fifteen ships at Cadiz, Orde's small squadron falling back on Cornwallis. Not until 18 April did Nelson hear at Palermo that the French had passed the straits. He told the ambassador that he was going west in chase: 'I am going out of the Mediterranean after the French fleet. It may be thought that I have protected too well Sardinia, Naples, Sicily, the Morea and Egypt from the French, but I feel that I have done right, and am therefore easy about any fate that may await me for having missed the French.' He now feared that Villeneuve would encounter Craig's force and at this stage of events he certainly intended sailing north from Gibraltar to join Cornwallis, but a foul wind kept him in the Mediterranean for another fortnight.

At Gibraltar on 6 May he met Commodore Donald Campbell, who was in command of a neutral Portuguese squadron from Lisbon. Campbell told him of strong rumours that the French had sailed west, not north, and in doing so lost his job as a neutral. In fact, Villeneuve reached Martinique on 14 May, only to find that Missiessy had returned to Rochefort and that there was no sign of Ganteaume.

When Nelson decided to stretch across to the West Indies he told the Admiralty that 'If they are not there, my squadron will be back again by the end of June – in short, before the enemy can know where I am'. The risk was enormous, and it seemed that half of Napoleon's plan had succeeded when Nelson was drawn westward; on the other hand, an unlocated fleet, which might turn up anywhere, certainly undermined Villeneuve's confidence as the weeks passed and he found himself with a fleet lacking in experience and without the support of Ganteaume's twenty-one ships.

On 4 June Nelson reached Barbados, where he was given the erroneous information that the enemy had gone south to Trinidad. He followed the false scent at the very moment that Villeneuve was moving north to Antigua, where on 10 June, his time being up, he turned east towards Europe. As Nelson followed north in pursuit he despatched the fast *Curieux* brig to England, suggesting that the French might be heading for Cadiz. Fortunately, she sighted the Combined Fleet in mid-ocean on a course which suggested a more northerly direction. Immediately on receipt of this information the eighty-year old Lord Barham (who replaced Melville as First Lord in May, when the latter was impeached for the malversation of Navy funds at an earlier date) ordered Cornwallis to detach the five ships blockading Rochefort to reinforce Calder off Ferrol. But when, on 22 July Villeneuve's thirteen ships encountered Calder's fifteen in thick weather off Cape Finisterre, the former was strong enough to brush past him to take refuge in Vigo bay with the loss of only two ships. When Nelson heard of the action he realized that the issue was still in doubt because the victory (as the English pleased to call it) may have been 'honourable to the parties concerned, but absolutely useless in the extended scale to bring Bonaparte to his marrow bones'.

Meanwhile Nelson reached Antigua on 14 June, four days after the French had left. It was by this narrow margin that he missed the encounter for which he had hoped over the past two years, though his presence in the West Indies prevented any interference with British possessions there, had the enemy so desired. Imagining that Villeneuve was making for Cadiz, he steered a more southerly course across the Atlantic to reach Gibraltar on 20 July. All that he found was Collingwood with four ships. The news that Craig's force had reached Malta was small comfort after such a long and unavailing chase. It was no thanks to him that the attention of the Admiralty had not been diverted, as Napoleon hoped, to the West Indies, so that the blockading shield was as strong as it was before these diversionary moves were made. In something like despair he fell back on Cornwallis, leaving eight ships with him and returning to Portsmouth with only the *Victory* and the *Superb*. A breathless note dated 18 August announced his arrival:

I am, my dearest Emma, this moment anchored and as the post will not go out till eight o'clock, I have ordered a Post Office express to tell you of my arrival. I hope we shall be out of quarantine tomorrow, when I shall fly to Merton. The boat is waiting and I must finish. God send us a happy meeting as our parting was sorrowful.

While Nelson was on leave at Merton Napoleon's invasion plans reached their peak. Ganteaume at Brest and Villeneuve at Ferrol were bombarded with orders to leave port. 'Lose not a a minute, but enter the Channel with my united fleets. England is ours; we are quite ready and everything is embarked. Come only for twenty-four hours and all is over.'

Villeneuve certainly did his best to obey. On 9 August he left Ferrol with twenty-nine ships of the line, sailing due west. His destination, 'according to circumstances', was either Brest or Cadiz, but he hoped to meet Allemand from Rochefort on his way. They missed each other in darkness off Cape Finisterre, Allemand continuing to Vigo and then turning into the Atlantic before he regained Rochefort without firing a shot. Villeneuve turned south for Cadiz on 15 August, when about a hundred and fifty kilometres (a hundred miles) west of Ferrol, the same day that Nelson joined Cornwallis on his way home. It was the crisis of the campaign, marking as it did the end of the invasion scheme. Fear of the strength of the force collected to the north of him (Cornwallis now had 36 ships at his disposal) was the fundamental reason for the decision to turn south, combined as it was with a lack of confidence in the ships under his command. As he told the Minister of Marine,

Seeing I had no confidence in the conditions of my ships, in their sailing, and in their ability to manoeuvre together, the concentration of the enemy and the knowledge they possess of all my movements since I reached the coast of Spain, leave me no hope of being able to fulfil the grand object for which the fleet was destined.

Nothing illustrates better than this confession the theory adumbrated by Joseph Le Maistre and later developed by Tolstoy that 'it is morale which loses battles, and it is morale which wins them. Battles which have changed the face of Europe were only lost because such and such a man believed they were lost.' At that very moment Villeneuve had his chance of success because Cornwallis committed what Napoleon called an *insigne bêtise* in the strategic disposition of his ships, and what is more, Barham approved. On 16 August he detached Calder with eighteen of the line and four frigates to guard Ferrol, thus weakening his force at the focal point off Ushant by sending half his fleet to a port from which the enemy had already sailed. Worse still, Calder on his own initiative took the potentially disastrous decision to continue south to Cadiz bay on 19 August. The French were already there, as Collingwood told his sister, 'in port like a forest. I reckon them now to be 36 sail of the line and plenty of frigates.'

This was the news which Blackwood, captain of the *Euryalus* frigate, brought to Merton on 2 September. Nelson was in London the previous day seeing the Prime Minister, who informed him of the probability that Villeneuve had reached Cadiz. 'Now, who is to take command?' asked Pitt.

'You cannot have a better man than the present one – Collingwood.'

'No, that won't do, you must command. Are you ready to sail in three days?'

'I am ready now', replied Nelson.

According to Emma, it was she who persuaded him to accept, adding that he said to her 'Brave Emma! If there were more Emmas there would be more Nelsons.' Apart from the fact that he had made the remark before, the version above, quoted on the authority of his brother-in-law, is a far more likely tale.

It was on 13 September that he left Emma and the five-year old Horatia for the last time. While he was changing horses on the Portsmouth road he wrote in his private diary: 'Friday night, at half-past ten, drove from dear, dear Merton, where I left all which I hold dear in this world, to go and serve my king and country.'

He had not been idle during the twenty-five days spent in England. Half the time he was in London seeing Barham at the Admiralty, Pitt at Downing Street, or visiting the Colonial Office, where he met Wellington on the occasion already referred to. He dined at the Ship Inn at Greenwich in the company of Sir Sidney Smith, of all people, with whom he had once quarrelled in the Mediterranean. Whenever he walked in the streets, his well-known appearance attracted crowds of people. Lord Minto met him in Piccadilly surrounded by a cheering mob: 'It is really quite affecting to see the wonder and admiration, and love and respect, of the whole world; and the genuine expression of all these sentiments at once, from gentle and simple, the moment he is seen.' Charles Lamb, no Nelson worshipper, saw him walking in Pall Mall, 'looking just as a Hero should look'.

The nation looked to him as a saviour and he was not slow in determining how their hopes might be realized. He kept turning over in his mind a mode of attack which would surprise and annihilate the enemy, once he was given the chance of meeting them. In conversation with Captain Keats at Merton he explained the germ of the tactical plan which was later communicated to his captains in the fleet.

'When we meet them, I'll tell you how I shall fight them. I shall form the Fleet in three Divisions in three Lines. One Division shall be composed of 12 or 14 of the fastest two-decked ships, which I shall always keep to windward, or in a situation of advantage; and I shall put them under an Officer who, I am sure, will employ them in the manner I wish, if possible. I consider it will be always in my power to throw them into Battle in any part I choose. . . . With the remaining part of the Fleet formed in two lines, I shall go at them at once, if I can, about one-third of their line from their leading ship. What do you think of it?' I paused. Seeing it, he said, 'But I'll tell you what I think of it. I think it will surprise and confound the Enemy. They won't know what I am about. It will bring forward a pell-mell Battle, and that is what I want.'

In the event, there were not three divisions but two, he himself commanding the windward or weather line, Collingwood the leeward, both to be led by flagships, which was unusual. Moreover, Nelson's column was heavily weighted in the van by three of the biggest ships – *Victory*, *Neptune*, *Téméraire* – the idea being that of a spear with which to break the enemy line. This highly original plan of attack was committed to paper soon after he joined the fleet as a Memorandum, dated 9 October, and its contents became known as the Nelson Touch. The document is so obscure in its wording, and so far removed from what actually occurred, that argument has raged ever since as to its interpretation. It is, however, the spirit rather than the letter of the Memorandum that counts. Collingwood's interpretation after the battle surely goes to the heart of the matter: 'Lord Nelson determined to substitute for exact order an impetuous attack in two distinct bodies. The weather line he commanded, and left the lee totally to my direction. He had assigned the points to be attacked.' With this general intention in mind, the vital sentence of the Memorandum is that 'No captain can do very wrong if he places his ship alongside that of an Enemy'.

Nelson left Portsmouth on 14 September. Making his way through the crowd gathered to see him embark from the George Inn, he said to Hardy 'I had their huzzas before – now I have

VIII   Nelson wounded at the Nile – engraving by Dubourg after Heath

IX   'Death of Nelson' – oil painting by D. Dighton

their hearts.' His reception by the fleet off Cadiz was equally flattering – 'the sweetest sensation of my life' –

I believe my arrival was most welcome not only to the comman-der of the Fleet, but also to every individual in it [he told Emma] and when I came to explain to them the Nelson touch it was like an electric shock. Some shed tears, all approved. 'It was new – it was singular – it was simple!' and from Admirals downwards, it was re-peated – 'It must succeed, if they ever allow us to get at them. You are, my Lord, surrounded by friends whom you inspire with con-fidence.'

Such was the genius of leadership. Villeneuve, on the other hand, though a pupil of the offensive-minded Suffren, could never bolster up the morale of a fleet which seemed to be per-petually on the run. He could echo Nelson's call to his officers by telling them that 'the captain who is not in action is not at his post', but when on the eve of action he signalled a reversal of course the comment of a Spanish captain summed up the general opinion: 'The fleet is doomed. The French admiral does not understand his business. He has compromised us all.' Even though he commanded 33 ships to Nelson's 27, morale was so low that he never had a chance of winning once battle was joined, however courageously individual ships were fought.

His reluctance to leave port is explained by this fact. It was the Emperor who forced him to put to sea. At the end of August Napoleon changed all his plans. On 23 August he told Talley-rand that if his fleets followed his instructions he would be 'master of England. But if my admirals hesitate I shall turn to the most urgent need. I strike my camps' – in order to march on Austria before she was prepared. This he did at Ulm, the day before Trafalgar.

The role of the Combined Fleet was also changed as the seat of war shifted to central Europe. It must go to Naples, and its commander-in-chief must be replaced by Rosily, an admiral who had not been to sea for many years. It was thus he, not Vil-leneuve, who compromised the fleet by forcing it into Nelson's arms. As soon as Villeneuve heard that his successor had reached

Madrid, and that Rear-Admiral Louis was watering five of Nelson's ships at Gibraltar, he determined to seize the chance to escape into the Mediterranean.

This was on 19 October. At noon that day, Cadiz bearing twenty kilometrees (twelve miles) E S E and Cape Trafalgar about fifteen kilometres (ten miles) further south, Nelson wrote his last letter.

My dearest Beloved Emma, the dear Friend of my Bosom,
The Signal has been made that the enemy's Combined Fleet are coming out of Port. We have very little wind, so that I have no hope of seeing them before tomorrow. May the God of Battles crown my endeavours with success; at all events, I will take care that my name shall ever be most dear to you and Horatia, both of whom I love as much as my own life.

The next day he continued to keep out of sight of the enemy, who were sailing on a S E course, in order to keep Villeneuve in ignorance of the size of the force opposing him. Advanced frigates kept him informed of the enemy's progress, which was very slow on account of the prevailing light airs. At four o'clock on the morning of 21 October Nelson ordered course N by E to cut off Villeneuve's line of retreat. At dawn, two hours later, the enemy were sighted fifteen kilometres to the eastward. According to one French observer, the English were first seen in line abreast. According to another, they were *sans ordre*. Soon they were seen to divide into two columns sailing roughly in line ahead. There being only a light wind, the process was so slow that it took six hours before they came within range. By 10.30 the groups 'merged into two columns, making the one [Nelson's] for the centre, and the other [Collingwood's] for the rear division'. In face of this slowly approaching menace, Villeneuve felt increasingly uncomfortable. His ships had lost steerage way, so there seemed little chance of reaching the Straits that day. For the second time he made a fatal move. At 0700 he signalled for the whole fleet to wear in succession in order to regain his base before it was too late. The consequence was, as Collingwood said, they now formed 'a curve, convexing to leeward, no longer a close-hauled line ahead but a ragged string of ships, some overlapping others'. Nelson's will had prevailed and the opportunity for annihilation was open to him. But Joseph Conrad, who, as a sailor, knew this part of the coast well, confessed himself aghast at the risk taken: had the treacherous wind failed or shifted, nothing in his opinion could have saved the leading ships from destruction.

Because of his death in battle we cannot know what precisely was in Nelson's mind. All we know is that he hoped for twenty prizes and that he left Collingwood to conduct the leeward column according to his own ideas, which were to break the line at the agreed point where Alava's flagship *Santa Ana* lay about half way from the rear ship. For those following the *Royal Sovereign* it was a case, as one young officer put it, of going down 'in no order, but every man to take his bird'. The process was agonizingly slow, requiring the strictest discipline during the approach. The scene on board the *Belleisle* immediately astern of Collingwood's flagship gives a vivid impression of those tense hours:

The silence on board was almost awful, broken only by the firm voice of the captain, 'Steady!' or 'Starboard a little!' which was repeated by the master to the quartermaster at the helm, and occasionally by an officer calling to the now impatient men: 'Lie down there, you, sir!' As we got nearer and nearer to the enemy the silence was, however, broken frequently by the sadly stirring shrieks of the wounded, for of them, and killed, we had more than fifty before we fired a shot; and our colours were three times shot away and rehoisted during the time. Seeing our men were fast falling, the first lieutenant ventured to ask Captain Hargood if he had not better show his broadside to the enemy and fire, if only to cover the ship with smoke. The gallant man's reply was somewhat stern but emphatic: 'No. We are ordered to go through the line, and go through she shall, by God!'

Nelson's account of his own approach includes the noble prayer which has since become famous:

At daylight, saw the Enemy's Combined Fleet from east to E S E; bore away; made the Signal for Order of Sailing and to Prepare for Battle. The Enemy with their heads to the southward. At seven the Enemy wearing in succession. May the Great God whom I worship, grant to my Country, and for the benefit of Europe in general, a great and glorious Victory; and may no misconduct in anyone tarnish it; and may humanity after Victory be the predominant feature in the British Fleet. For myself, individually, I commit my life to Him who made me, and may His blessing light upon my endeavours for serving my Country faithfully. To Him I resign myself, and the just cause which is entrusted to me to defend. Amen, Amen, Amen.

Having added a codicil to his will leaving Emma as 'a legacy to my king and country, that they will give her ample provision to maintain her rank in life', he visited every deck before going up to the poop. He was wearing the full dress uniform of a Vice-Admiral of the White, with four Orders on his breast. Hardy remonstrated that this made him unnecessarily conspicuous, but it was entirely in character for him to refuse such advice. Once he had satisfied himself that everything was in order, he told Blackwood 'I'll now amuse the Fleet with a signal'. Summoning Pasco, the signal lieutenant, he said he wished to make the signal ENGLAND CONFIDES THAT EVERY MAN WILL DO HIS DUTY. Pasco pointed out that Popham's Marine Dictionary, a new method of signalling in which numeral flags denoted letters or words, the word 'confides' did not occur. Might he substitute 'expects'? 'That will do, Pasco, make it directly.' The famous signal was then made in twelve hoists:

253 (England) 269 (Expects) 863 (That) 261 (Every) 471 (Man) 958 (Will) 220 (Do) 370 (His) 4 (D) 21 (U) 19 (T) 24 (Y)

Collingwood's reaction, as he munched an apple to pass the time, was typically phlegmatic: he wished Nelson would not make any more signals, for they all knew what they had to do. 'Now, gentlemen,' he told his officers, 'let us do something today which the world may talk of hereafter.' A few minutes later, at 11.45, he struck at the *Santa Ana*, the thirteenth ship from the rear. As he did so, the *Fougueux* moved up, but when

The Battle of Trafalgar

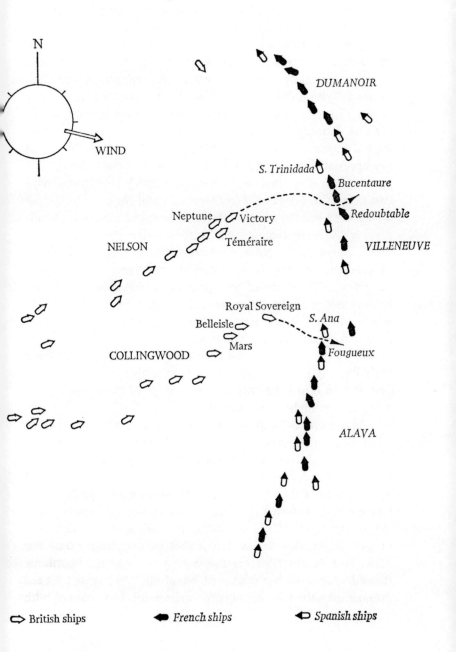

N

WIND

DUMANOIR

S. Trinidada

Bucentaure

Redoubtable

Neptune Victory

NELSON Téméraire VILLENEUVE

Royal Sovereign

S. Ana

Belleisle

Mars

COLLINGWOOD Fougueux

ALAVA

British ships French ships Spanish ships

she saw that the *Royal Sovereign* was about to carry away her bowsprit she backed topsails to engage the two following English ships, *Belleisle* and *Mars*, with such devastating effect that the latter was totally dismasted and her captain killed.

'See how that noble fellow Collingwood carries his ship into action,' exclaimed Nelson as eight ships of the lee division engaged sixteen opponents. It was twenty minutes later before his own division came into action. What makes the track chart of the *Victory* so extraordinary is that it seems to flout all the laws of gunnery. When ships fired broadside it was of fundamental importance to avoid 'having the T crossed', that is to say approaching at right angles ships which could bring fifty guns to bear simultaneously. Yet the *Victory* (104 guns), with two other three-deckers *Téméraire* (98) and *Neptune* (98) close on her stern quarters, appears to have done just that. With bands playing 'Rule, Britannia' and 'Britons Strike Home', she bore slowly down on the red-and-white striped *Santissima Trinidada* of 120 guns. As the Spanish flagship and the French flagship *Bucentaure* (80) astern of her opened fire, Nelson altered course to pass astern of the latter, though by that time the *Victory's* wheel and mizzen topmast had been shot away and some fifty men had been killed or wounded on deck. At 12.04, runs the master's log, 'open'd fire on the enemy's van in passing down their line. At 12.20 in attempting to pass through the enemy's line, fell on board the 10th and 11th ships of the enemy's line, when the action became general.'

The eleventh ship was the *Redoutable*, a two-decker of 74 guns under Captain Lucas. She was the best trained ship in the fleet and she now pushed up so close to the *Bucentaure* that her bowsprit touched her taffrail. Nelson ordered the helm hard aport, telling Hardy 'I cannot help it: it does not signify which one we run on board of – take your choice'. As the *Victory* thrust through the line, her 68-lb carronade shattered the stern of the *Bucentaure* and a double-shotted broadside raked her deck. Equally terrible was the execution done on board the *Redoubtable* with her starboard broadside. With yards locked inextricably, the two ships drifted to leeward. The crews of both stood ready to board, the upper decks being almost cleared by musketry and grapeshot fired by both sides. At 01.35 a sharpshooter in the tops of the *Redoutable* shot Nelson at a range of only fifteen metres. As he fell he cried out 'They have done for me at last, Hardy. My backbone is shot through.' He was carried below to the surgeon's cockpit, covering his face with a handkerchief so that his men should not be discouraged.

During the four hours he lay dying the battle raged around him. Every ship in the fleet, with the exception of one or two in the extreme rear, found an opponent. As Nelson had foreseen, the impact of his three-deckers so disorganized the enemy that victory had been gained before Dumanoir's van could tack to the assistance of the disordered centre and rear. To their discredit, some of the van ships refused to obey their admiral's signal and ran for Cadiz. His counter-attack with four ships was therefore easily beaten off and he continued southward to escape the fate which overtook the remainder of his comrades.

Before Nelson died the day was won. Villeneuve and two of his flag officers were prisoners. Of the 33 ships which left port, only 11 returned; 17 others lay so badly damaged they were driven ashore by the storm which blew up after the battle was over; 13 others were in the hands of prize crews and the *Achille*, like *L'Orient* at the Nile, exploded in flames as a funeral pyre of French hopes for mastery at sea. Of Nelson's 27 ships many, including the *Victory*, suffered serious damage, but most of them were soon off Cadiz again to resume the blockade. The disparity in casualties is the best indication of the nature of the victory: 450 lost their lives in Nelson's fleet, some 4,700, apart from prisoners, in Villeneuve's.

Nelson's last words were noted by Dr Beatty, the surgeon of the *Victory*.

'Don't throw me overboard, Hardy.'
'Oh no, certainly not.'
'Then you know what to do; and take care of my dear Lady Hamilton. Take care of poor Lady Hamilton. Kiss me, Hardy. Now I am satisfied. Thank God, I have done my duty.'

'Partial firing continued until 4.30,' runs the ship's log, 'when a victory having been reported to the Right Honourable Lord Viscount Nelson K B and Commander-in-chief, he then died of his wound.'

Lieutenant Lapenotière brought the news of Trafalgar to the Admiralty at one o'clock on the morning of 6 November. The aged First Lord was aroused to send copies of Collingwood's despatch to the proper quarters, including *The Times* newspaper. When John Barrow, Second Secretary of the Admiralty, arrived for work a few hours later he was greeted by the First Secretary with the words 'Glorious news! The most glorious victory our brave navy has ever achieved – but Nelson is dead.'

This was the attitude of the people of London. As Lord Malmesbury said, 'I never saw so little public joy.' The nation had been confident that if the fleets met the British would triumph, but the death of Nelson was never contemplated. Nor were the fruits of his victory evident for some time. It was obvious that the danger of invasion was past, but the Grand Army marched through Europe from victory to victory. Pitt died a few days after Nelson's funeral, burdened by a sense of failure. Once Napoleon had conquered the continent, once the Treaty of Tilsit with the Czar put him in a position to turn upon the last enemy, there followed a contest between land and sea power such as we have witnessed in the present century.

Napoleon's attempts to strangle British commerce in order to bring her to her knees involved closing the entire European coastline to her trade. This meant the occupation of Denmark and Portugal. But the supremacy at sea which had been won by Nelson enabled Britain to make a pre-emptive strike against Denmark in 1807 and to land her first successful army in the Peninsula in the following year. The seas around Europe were

patrolled by British cruisers, her blockading fleets kept the remains of the French navy in harbour and as a consequence of
her control of the periphery amphibious expeditions could be
launched on a grand scale at what ever point she chose. True,
the Walcheren expedition was another dismal failure, but the
star of Wellington slowly brightened in the Peninsula. When
the people of Spain rose against the French, their example was
followed in wars of liberation all over the Continent as the
Grand Army found itself converted into a corps of policemen
and customs officers in order to deprive the subject nations of
their freedom and their prosperity. In the end, the advantages
conferred by supremacy at sea proved superior to the consequences of military and political power on the continent. It is
significant that the last Napoleon ever saw of Europe was the
island of Ushant, off which blockading fleets had continued to
cruise for the ten years which succeeded Trafalgar.

After the victory, Nelson's body was conveyed back to Spithead in a cask of brandy. It was so well preserved that a death
mask could be taken and the fatal ball extracted from the spine,
to be preserved to this day at Windsor Castle. The *Victory* continued to the Nore, where the body was put into a leaden coffin
which was encased in the wooden coffin made from the mast of
L'Orient, which Ben Hallowell had given Nelson after the battle
of the Nile. On Christmas Eve this was landed at the Royal
Hospital, Greenwich, where it lay in state in the Painted Hall
for a few days, during which some thirty thousand people paid
their respects to the dead hero.

On 8 January it was taken up river to the Admiralty in a
procession of boats for the funeral next day. It was the grandest
occasion of its kind which London had ever seen. The fine frosty
weather brought out the crowds in tens of thousands. The naval
contingent accompanying the black plumed funeral car consisted of thirty-one admirals, a hundred captains, forty-eight
men of the *Victory's* crew and forty-eight Greenwich pen-
sioners who had fought under Nelson's command. Among the
crowds which lined the route from Charing Cross to St Paul's
two individuals may be instanced: a boy, Frederick Marryat,

who after twenty years at sea was to immortalize the naval war in his novels; and the sad figure of Villeneuve and his flag captain. Two months later, the defeated admiral was to return to France, where he committed suicide.

At St Paul's the coffin was lowered into a black basalt sarcophagus which Cardinal Wolsey had once ordered for himself and which had been left at Windsor for centuries. When the huge, shot-torn ensign of the *Victory* covering the coffin was removed, the members of the crew who were present tore it in pieces to preserve mementoes of their dead leader. Today the tomb lies in the crypt next to the granite sarcophagus made for the Duke of Wellington, and it is flanked by memorials to the two captains killed at Trafalgar. There, among the monuments to admirals such as Rodney, Duncan and St Vincent, Nelson rests in the cathedral where he always hoped to lie.

Two notable absentees from the funeral were Lady Nelson and Lady Hamilton. Parliament was generous to the former and to Nelson's family : she received a pension of £2,000 a year, each of the sisters received £1,500, and the Rev. William (now Earl) Nelson, £99,000 for the purchase of the Trafalgar estate near Salisbury and a grant of £5,000 a year 'for ever'. In 1946 this grant to a family which never did the state much service was suspended.

Neither Emma Hamilton nor Horatia ever received a penny from the public purse. In the final codicil to his will Nelson had left the former as 'a legacy to the nation'. Hardy faithfully delivered the charge, but it never got further than Pitt, who died a few days later. Neither the Prince Regent nor Grenville, the new Prime Minister were inclined to honour Nelson's dying request, nor was the Rev. William Nelson. Since Emma never had any idea about money and continued her extravagant way of living, she was soon seriously in debt. For a time she was imprisoned, until she fled to Calais, where she died in very distressed circumstances in 1815. 'For some time before she died', wrote Horatia, then aged fourteen, 'she was not kind to me, but she had much to try her, also to spite her, and I was too well aware of the state of her finances, so much so that I applied to

Lord Nelson to advance me a portion of my dividend for use in providing for necessaries for the house.'

The tragic circumstances in which Horatia was brought up may be appreciated by recalling Nelson's last letter to her when she was five years old.

My dearest Angel. I rejoice to hear that you are so very good a girl, and love my dear Lady Hamilton, who most dearly loves you. Give her a kiss from me. The Combined Fleets of the Enemy are now reported to be coming out of Cadiz. . . . Receive, my dearest Horatia, the affectionate Parental Blessing of your Father.

While she always knew that Nelson was her father, she never regarded Emma as otherwise than a guardian. As soon as she was freed from subservience to that pathetic drink-sodden figure, she enjoyed the protection of the Matcham family until she married the Reverend Philip Ward. Thereafter, as Mrs Nelson-Ward, she lived the life of a country parson's wife until she died at the age of eighty-one. She is described on her tombstone as 'the adopted daughter of Lord Nelson'. It was not until his intimate letters to Emma were printed by Alfred Morrison in 1893 that the identity of her mother, so long suspected and so carefully evaded by Victorian admirers, was put beyond a doubt.

The lustre of Nelson's fame during the next generation was overshadowed by the prominence of the Duke of Wellington, as a general and later as a statesman. It was kept alive by the popularity of Southey's biography published in 1813 as an expansion of a review in the *Quarterly* of the ponderous official life by Clarke and McArthur. John Murray printed a series of cheap editions which gave this 'eulogy of our great naval hero', as Southey called it, a wide circulation. Generations of boys have been reared on it and in the United States Navy it was made official reading for young officers.

The quarry from which all subsequent biographies have been hewn was the edition of his Letters and Despatches in seven volumes which Sir Harris Nicolas published between 1844 and 1846. This great monument of scholarship remains, as its editor claimed, 'the most genuine and truthful portrait of a

Public Character that the world has ever seen'. It was much more than a rival to the volumes of Wellington's despatches printed ten years earlier because, by including every personal letter which the editor could lay his hands on, it presents a rounded portrait of the man both in his personal and public capacity. It achieved a wide sale, so that Nelson was accorded his proper place as the national hero of the Pax Britannica which now prevailed, mainly on account of his efforts. It is to Nicolas's assiduity that we also owe many of the Nelson relics, in particular the Trafalgar uniform which he persuaded the Prince Consort to purchase and to present to the Royal Hospital at Greenwich, where the core of the collection now in the National Maritime Museum originated.

'The tardy manifestation of the national gratitude by the erection of a monument to Nelson in the Metropolis of the Empire', remarked Nicolas, 'is very discreditable to the Country.' Discussions about such a monument had begun thirty years earlier and meanwhile many provincial cities had erected memorials of one sort or another. Overlooking Portsmouth there was a pillar, and overlooking Edinburgh a churn-shaped tower from the top of which a time ball dropped to mark the hour of noon, when the gun was fired from the Castle on the other side of the town; so well synchronized were these signals that one Scotsman was heard to say 'Mon, that's guid shooting.' At Dublin William Wilkins, the architect of the National Gallery, designed a pillar which has since been destroyed.

Meanwhile, adjacent to the old Admiralty buildings, Nash began to lay out Trafalgar Square (as yet unnamed) in 1826. Among the mass of mews and stables then covering the site, Wilkins's National Gallery was built to overlook it. Trafalgar Square was completed by Barry and so named in 1835, soon after which a Nelson Memorial Committee was formed for the design of a central monument. Barry opposed the erection of a column, which he thought would spoil the elevation of Wilkins's elegant building, but as subscriptions slowly came in work was commenced on a design by William Railton in 1839. All that the government did was to provide a site: the column itself was built by public subscription, just as the *Victory* was saved at a later date. It is a fluted column, 75 metres (245 feet) high, of Devon granite, and the capital (a fact that is seldom realized) is cast from iron guns from Woolwich Arsenal. Surmounting the column is the universally known statue by E. H. Baily, placed in position in 1843, the year before Nicolas's literary monument helped to raise the funds. The four bas-reliefs on the pedestal which commemorate Nelson's four victories are cast from guns captured at those battles. Later additions were the four magnificent lions modelled by Landseer in 1867, and the two fountains backed by busts of Jellicoe and Beatty installed in the square by Sir Edwin Lutyens in 1939.

A personal link which carried Nelson's fame and influence forward for another half century is Admiral Lord Fisher. He took enormous pride in the fact that he was the last midshipman to be nominated by the last of Nelson's captains at the instance of Nelson's niece in 1854. His first ship was the *Victory* and as a young officer he waded through Nicolas's volumes to acquire a few Nelsonian tags which he loved to repeat on every occasion when he rose to a position which enabled him to revive the efficiency of Nelson's navy. Fisher was a remarkable mixture of the reformer and the traditionalist. At one moment he was saying that History is a collection of exploded ideas, and at the next he was asking himself, What would Nelson do now? His Nelsonian information (as has been the case with many distinguished admirals, to judge from their speeches at the annual Trafalgar Night dinners still held in the Painted Hall) was superficial, but sufficient to be turned to whatever use happened to be uppermost in his mind. When he threatened to 'Copenhagen' the Kaiser's navy, he was confusing the events of 1801 with those of 1807, and when he made a point of joining the Admiralty as First Naval Lord on Trafalgar Day 1904 to initiate his great reforms, he took up his duties a day too soon. But even when he was designing the *Dreadnought*, the most revolutionary ship of that epoch, he found time to contemplate a centennial tribute and to compile a Nelson anthology which still remains in typescript. This curious compilation concludes by pointing to another of Nelson's avowed disciples. Quoting Nelson's remark 'Close with a Frenchman, but out-manoeuvre a Russian', he comments: 'This is E X A C T L Y what Togo did! And so we might call Togo "Nelson's Servile Copyist", meaning no disparagement of Togo.'

The Japanese victory at Tsushima in 1905 so closely resembled Trafalgar in its completeness that the illusion of the Big Battle by which all wars at sea were to be won was to have deleterious consequences in 1914. Not only the Japanese, but the German, British and American navies were bred on Mahan's thesis that the annihilation of the enemy battle fleet was the primary objective in naval warfare. The idea was fortified by Mahan's influential biography of Nelson as 'the Embodiment of Sea Power', which was published in 1897. It was further strengthened by the enormous literature which appeared at the time of the Trafalgar centenary celebrations.

Even more important than those manifestations of Nelsonian idolatry was the official Report of a Committee appointed by the Admiralty to examine and consider the evidence relating to the tactics employed at the battle which was printed in 1913. The Navy which entered the First World War was thus saturated not only by a century of Nelson tradition but by studies of his tactics, in spite of the fact that a complete revolution in the design of ships and guns had occurred in the interval. To Admiral Richmond, the best historian the Navy ever produced, this failure to appreciate the true lessons of history and this misreading of Nelson's example was both frightening and exasperating. What could one say, for example, to Sir Doveton Sturdee, Chief of Staff in the Channel Fleet at the outbreak of war, who, when asked for stronger protection against minelayers, replied 'Impossible. Nelson never did such a thing as to break up a squadron.'

It was all very well for Fisher to groom Jellicoe as 'the future Nelson', but at the same time he sanctified two dangerous and most un-Nelsonian traditions, the two 'fetishes' which Professor Marder has shown to have done so much damage to British planning about the war at sea. These were the concept of a rigid line of battle and the centralization of command which hampered the fleet so seriously at the battle of Jutland. Jellicoe had never even read Mahan, but if he had had a staff which read history critically he might have been told that Nelson never approved of a rigid line, and that the whole point of his preparations for the Nile and Trafalgar was to leave his subordinates sufficient freedom of decision within the general plan to use their ships to the best advantage on their own initiative.

The real Nelson Touch was defined by the more percipient Joseph Conrad. Writing in 1906, when steam had driven sail from the seas and as a retired master mariner turned novelist, he suggested that Nelson's real importance lay in his example of leadership.

Through the fidelity of his fortune and the power of his inspiration, he stands unique among the leaders of fleets and sailors. He brought heroism into the line of duty. Verily he is a terrible ancestor. . . . To be so great and to remain so accessible to the affection of one's fellowmen is the mark of exceptional humanity.

Though Nelson's ghost may have been exorcized by new forms of sea and air power, his personal and spiritual example remains. 'Who is there of his time,' asked Fisher, 'or indeed of any other time, that still lives in our memories as he does?' Both as a man and as the principal architect of British supremacy at sea in the nineteenth century, he remains rooted in the affections and the admiration of his countrymen.

Appendix I

Rates of Ships

Rate	Number of guns	Weight of broadside (lb)	Complement	Tonnage	Length of Lower Gun Deck (ft)
1st rate	100 and over	2500	850–950	2000–2600	180
2nd rate	98	2300	750	2000	180
	90	2050	750	2000	170
3rd rate	80	1974	720	2000	
	74	1764	640	1700	170–160
	60	1200	490	1300	
4th rate	50	800	350	1100	150
5th rate	44				
	40				
	38	636–350	320–215	900–700	150–130
	36				
	32				
6th rate	28				
	24	250–180	200–160	650–550	130–120
	20				

Appendix II

The Appropriation of Men at Quarters
HMS *Victory* 1805

Deck	No. of guns on each deck		No. of men on each deck	No. of men to each gun and its 'opposite'
Quarter Deck	12	12-pdrs	60	10
Forecastle	2	12-pdrs		
	2	68-lb carronades	20	10
Main Deck	30	12-pdrs	150	10
Middle Deck	28	24-pdrs	168	12
Lower Deck	30	32-pdrs	225	15
TOTAL	104		623	

IN ADDITION

Small Arms	10	
Main Top	3	
Fore Top	2	
Mizzen Top	2	
Rigging	11	
Attend Signals	6	
Grand Magazine	25	For duty in the Magazine
After Magazine	7	and to hand powder
Hanging Magazine	16	along the passages
Fore Hatchway	7	To whip up, or to hand
Main Hatchway	4	powder from these
After Hatchway	8	hatchways
Boatswain's Store	1	
Gunner's Store	1	
Carpenter's Store	1	
Purser's Store	1	
Helm	5	
Well and Wings	6	
Cockpit	6	

TOTAL NO. OF MEN QUARTERED	745
Number of Officers	24
Mates, Midshipmen and Clerks	33
Number of Boys	40
Number of 'Widows' Men'	8

TOTAL COMPLEMENT	850

List of Books

The principal source of information remains the seven-volume edition of Sir Harris Nicolas's *Despatches and Letters of Lord Nelson* (1844-6). To this should be added Alfred Morrison's *Hamilton and Nelson Papers* (1893) and *Nelson's Letters to his Wife*, edited by George P. Naish for the Navy Records Society in 1958. The same Society has also printed the logs of his actions in *Logs of the Great Sea Fights*, ed. Sturges Jackson (1900). See also Desbrière, E., *Campaign of Trafalgar* (1907) and Corbett, Sir Julian, *Campaign of Trafalgar* (1910).

Among the many biographies of Nelson the most valuable are those by Robert Southey (1813), A. T. Mahan (1897), Clennell Wilkinson (1931), Carola Oman (1947) and Oliver Warner (1958).

A useful guide to the extensive Nelson literature is by Oliver Warner, *Lord Nelson: A Guide to Reading, with a Note on Contemporary Portraits* (Caravel Press, 1955).

Index

Index